Items brought back from early times in Palestine and Israel. The covering is a *keffiyeh*, a traditional Palestinian head covering. The small bowl, lamp, candlesticks, and box are olive wood creations made by Ramallah woodcarver Kort with designs by Ramallah artist Badran. The olive wood camel is one brought home by Great-Aunt Annice Carter. From left to right, the mugs are a traditional Palestinian ceramic design, a mug from the Israeli peace community of Wahat al-Salam/Neve Shalom, and glass made by traditional Hebron glass blowers. The photo in back is of the Ramallah city center as it looked in 1954—and still looked much the same in 1970.

Palestine and Israel
A Personal Encounter

Max L. Carter

BARCLAY PRESS
Newberg, OR 97132

Palestine and Israel
A Personal Encounter
©2020 by Max L. Carter

All rights reserved. No part may be reproduced
for any commercial purpose by any method without
permission in writing from the copyright holder.

Barclay Press, Inc.
Newberg, Oregon
www.barclaypress.com

Cover and interior design: Mareesa Fawver Moss.
Printed in the United States of America.

ISBN 978-1-59498-067-1

This book is dedicated to my students at the Ramallah Friends School who taught me far more than I taught them. It is also dedicated to my wife, Jane, who has accompanied me on this encounter with Palestine and Israel, falling in love with the people and the land as I have—and loving me through it all.

Table of Contents

Introduction 9
Chapter 1: First Impressions 13
Chapter 2: Occasional Activity 43
Chapter 3: The First Intifada 59
Chapter 4: Between the Intifadas 81
Chapter 5: The Second Intifada, Part 1 91
Chapter 6: The Second Intifada, Part 2 103
Chapter 7: The Second Intifada, Part 3 123
Afterword 149

Introduction

Growing up on a farm in Indiana, I never imagined that most of my adult life would be affected more by the Mideast than by the American Midwest! All I knew of the Middle East was what I'd read in the Bible. Of course, that slim knowledge gleaned from a book nearly 2,000 years old was hardly an adequate preparation for what I would encounter during my adult years, but I am deeply grateful for the experience. Without it, I wouldn't be the person I am today; would not have met some of my closest friends—including my wife; would not have developed a career path that was so rewarding; indeed, my whole life has been changed completely by what began in 1970 with my first experience in Palestine and Israel.

Had it not been for the military draft and the U.S. war in Vietnam, that encounter would not have happened. In 1964, I had committed myself to conscientious objection to participation in war or the preparation for war. It was a combination of my Quaker upbringing, Christian commitment, and an encounter with a survivor of the atomic bomb blast in Hiroshima. In 1966, I turned 18 and applied for conscientious objector status with the Selective Service System. Having had the good foresight to be born in a Hoosier county chock full of Quakers, Mennonites, Brethren, and Amish—members of the historic peace churches—I was granted C.O. status by my draft board with no difficulty.

That was also the year I enrolled in college, and armed with my student deferment from the draft and my own commitment to volunteer for alternative service as a C.O. when I graduated from college, I had the luxury of researching where I might do my alternative service. I knew I wanted to use my undergraduate preparation for a teaching career, to use my service in the cause of peacemaking, and to serve in a region where there was conflict. The Quaker schools in Ramallah, a town in the Israeli-occupied West Bank, fit the bill.

I had learned of the Ramallah schools—a girls school founded in 1869 and a boys school begun in 1901—through the service of my Great-Aunt Annice Carter. She first went to Ramallah in the 1920s to teach at the Friends Girls School, eventually becoming the principal of FGS and working there a total of fourteen years before retiring in 1965. Her letters home were read by my grandfather to our family gatherings. Other than thinking it sounded quite romantic (an idea I would later become disabused of), I didn't pay any attention to Ramallah until I considered teaching there as an option for my service.

Indeed, I finally selected teaching in Ramallah and learned that there were positions open, and the Friends Boys School was interested in hiring me. Again, my draft board gave me no difficulty, telling me I could select the location of my alternative service and approving FBS as my site.

The following pages reflect my experience of falling in love with the people and place of Palestine and my growing understanding of the impact of Israel's victory in the 1967 war and occupation of Arab lands. My narrative covers those first two years of teaching from 1970 to 1972 and subsequent visits to the region, leading groups, and on study trips. This collection covers the time from 1970 through the second Intifada (the Palestinian uprising against Israel's military occupation), ending in 2005.

The source materials for these reflections come from aerograms (remember those?) I sent home during my teaching stint and journals kept during subsequent trips, along with my somewhat sketchy memory. I am especially indebted to my wife Jane and our daughter Maia for their keen memories and copious notes taken on some joint ventures. It is my hope that readers will find some insight into the issues in the Palestinian-Israeli situation through my engagement with—and reflection on—those issues.

I am grateful to all those people who helped make these experiences possible—even my draft board! My late mother was a constant source of support and love, always placing me in a "prayer bubble" when I traveled to the Middle East. After I married Jane in 1974, she became another constant source of love and support, herself falling in love with Palestine after our first trip to Ramallah together in 1979. Eventually, all three of our children also experienced the region, one daughter later doing her own two years of teaching at the Ramallah Friends School (the successor to the former Friends Girls and Boys Schools), developing an academic career in Middle East politics and international peacemaking, and introducing her own husband and three children to the area.

And of course, I owe a tremendous debt of gratitude to the staff and students of the Ramallah Friends School and the staff of Friends United Meeting (FUM), the international Quaker organization that oversees the work of Quaker education in Ramallah. Those people are too numerous to mention, but many of their names appear in the following pages.

I also owe great thanks to those who endured reading through the draft manuscript of this compilation, making important suggestions and correcting my numerous errors. My good wife, Jane, familiar with my penchant for error during our nearly forty-five years of marriage, gave it a good editing, as did editor and friend Paula Hampton.

Inshallah (God willing), my experience as reflected in these pages might encourage some others to explore Palestine and Israel for themselves—either by further reading or by visiting in person. (I know someone who takes groups annually.)

Chapter 1: First Impressions

When my Great-Aunt Annice Carter, a veteran of fourteen years in Ramallah, saw me off at the Indianapolis airport in 1970 for my two-year stint of teaching in Palestine, she had this stern advice for me: "Max, the Carters have a good name in Ramallah. Don't ruin it!" Nearly fifty years later, the jury is still out on what damage I've done to the family name and Annice's good reputation.

I did not travel directly to Ramallah that August of '70. Since I was going to be in the neighborhood of Europe, I had been named a delegate by my Quaker community, Western Yearly Meeting of Friends, to attend the triennial gathering of the Friends World Committee for Consultation in Sigtuna, Sweden.

To rural Hoosiers, Scandinavia is on the way to the Middle East.

But I was delighted to have the opportunity to mix and mingle with Quakers from around the world. It was my first experience with such an array of Friends from different nationalities and backgrounds, including some of the Quaker luminaries of that era: Douglas Steere, Elise and Kenneth Boulding; Ranjit Chetsingh; Heberto Sein, William Barton, T. Canby Jones, Duncan Wood, and many others.

I wrote home to express my amazement at the dominant spiritual drive of the conference from East African Quakers and my opportunities to speak with East German Quakers and learn of their impressions of life under Communist control. One East German I spoke with described how, indeed, the West Germans were ahead of them economically and had fewer restrictions on their freedoms, but he was content where he was and believed the Berlin Wall had to be built to keep young workers from fleeing and compromising the ability to grow the economy.

The time in Sigtuna also provided me with my first introduction to Palestinian Quakers in the person of Jean and Fuad Zaru, who would be a significant presence in my life over the next two years and indeed, for many decades. In my first letter home, I shared my impressions of meeting with Jean:

> Jean and I have had several long talks about the Middle East situation. She tells me not to worry about a thing, since the American Consulate will take care of me. What she asks is, "Who is going to take care of the Palestinians?"

I went on to share how Jean explained perceptions of American thought on the Middle East. "The U.S. will send soldiers to a foreign country to fight against a philosophy (Communism) and justify that, yet they will side with Israel and condemn the Arabs for fighting in their own country for their own land. Is it right," she asked, "for the world to give Israel the land that they possessed for seventy years 2,000 years ago and take it away from the Palestinians who had held it for 2,000 years until 1948?"

I noted how my thinking on the situation in the Middle East was already being challenged.

After a week in Germany following the conference, I finally arrived in Ramallah, sending my first letter home from Palestine on August 28. I shared about my first visit to Jerusalem to see the holy sites and commented on the constant cycle of visits in homes and the overwhelming hospitality of tea, sweets, and local specialties; I also noted that my teaching load would be two English classes and four math classes for a total of twenty-nine periods a week—all different preparations. The big excitement I reported, though, was a cholera outbreak. "Nothing to worry about," I wrote; "we are boiling our water and not buying fruit."

The first mention I made of the military or political situation was brief: "There are few signs of the war here. I see an occasional army patrol with their helmets and guns, and each night jets fly over on their way to attack in Jordan. There hasn't been any trouble in Ramallah since March."

It wasn't long before my students were teaching me about the situation. In early September, several airplanes were hijacked by two Palestinian organizations and flown to Jordan and Egypt. While I was supervising recess on the playground, three of my students approached and asked what I thought of the hijacking. I gave the kind of answer one would expect from a Quaker conscientious objector, and the three boys responded, "We don't want anyone harmed either; we don't really want any violence. But how do we get the world to pay attention to Palestinian concerns when even the prime minister of Israel, Golda Meir, has recently been quoted as saying, 'There is no such thing as a Palestinian'? The world seems to pay attention only to violence, so we have to use violence. Still, we hope nobody is hurt."

Talking with students was, in fact, my main source of information—that and the nightly BBC radio broadcasts. Initially, though, I was so consumed by organizing classes and coping with the overwhelming work load that there wasn't much time to be concerned with politics. That was soon to change.

In a letter home on September 16, I wrote, "Life is going on fairly normally here, although I can imagine what it sounds like back home. . . . Conditions in Jordan are deteriorating, and guerrillas have occupied areas of Jordan. General sentiment in Ramallah seems to favor the guerrillas. My students, especially, are hoping that King Hussein will be ousted and the Popular Front for the Liberation of Palestine invested as the new government."

The letter went on to note that the populace had remained calm even while Israel had arrested more than 450 alleged guerrilla supporters or relatives, following the plane hijackings. I probably didn't ease my mother's worries by stating, "If the situation worsens and the U.S. Consulate orders all Americans out, my housemate Donn and I will be staying. . . . The Board on Missions has decided that the single men in Ramallah should stay and take care of the property owned by the American Quaker organization."

By the time of my next missive, Black September, the pitched battle between King Hussein's forces and the guerrillas of the Palestine Liberation Organization (PLO) had erupted. I shared that the situation was a powder keg but that I would be OK as long as the United States or Israel didn't intervene. "If they do," I wrote, "the commandoes have promised to wipe out American interests in the Middle East."

Students at the school, however, continued to be on friendly terms with me, understanding my Quaker views and asking only that I understand their problems. Nearly everyone in Ramallah had relatives in Jordan, and they were deeply concerned for their safety as the fighting escalated. Jets continued to scream overhead; columns of smoke could be seen rising from across the distant Jordan Valley. Students stayed up all night glued to their radios for news, and one day the eleventh grade class didn't come to school as a show of solidarity with those suffering in the war. My tenth grade class remained silent one day during an entire math period while I continued my lecture, telling me later it was in commemoration of their relatives in Jordan about whom they had no information.

With little reliable news, rumors ran wild. It was heard that bodies filled the streets, that Amman was nearly leveled, that 30,000 had been killed, and that it was nothing short of a genocide against the Palestinian people. I wrote, "My students ask me how they can concentrate on school while this was on their minds. It is difficult for me to stand in front of the class and tell them that $a + c = b + c$ means $a = b$. It just doesn't apply to their situation!"

"It is really touching," I said, "to look out on a class and see 15-year olds with tears in their eyes and trembling chins. . . . I am not fearful about my situation," I went on. "How can I be when I realize these people are here for life?"

My letter of September 26 continued the disturbing news. "It is impossible to teach. Most of my classes have been out on strike all week. . . . Teachers break down in tears. We have spent the past few days preparing the school campuses to receive refugees from the fighting. Classrooms and dining rooms have been filled with beds—seventy in the Girls School. Nobody has arrived yet, though." As it turned out, no refugees did arrive.

I ended my letter by sharing my growing sense of sympathy with the plight of the Palestinians. "They are so hungry for someone to understand their problems. The Arabs have rejected them (witness their treatment in Jordan); the West has rejected them. They are so frustrated. I am afraid events will lead either to continued persecution of the Palestinians or a blow-up. The hardest thing about it all, though, is not to be able to do anything, except understand them."

A piece of that understanding came with the September 28 issue of *Time Magazine*. One morning I came into my first class of the day to find all the students huddled around my desk, looking excitedly at the magazine. The cover depicted a Palestinian fighter in traditional *keffiyeh* (head covering), carrying a Kalashnikov rifle against a green background with several lines of Arabic words. Today I can read them: Al-Khalil, Halhoul, Akka, Kafr Qasim, and others—names of Palestinian towns and cities, some the victims of a massacre of its residents (Kafr Qasim) and others, like Akka, where Palestinians had to flee in the '48 war. The students recognized the names of villages their families had fled, even though these young people were born after the events of the *Nakba* ("the catastrophe," Palestinians' word for their loss of land and homes in the creation of the modern state of Israel). There were tears in their eyes as they experienced a recognition, finally, of their suffering and resistance.

Only a week after my arrival in Ramallah, Palestinian hijackers had flown four airplanes into the Jordanian and Egyptian deserts and blown them up (after all passengers and crew were evacuated). The next week, Black September erupted in Jordan. No sooner had that fighting diminished than my letter of September 30 carried the news of my next "welcome to Palestine!" event: the death of Egyptian president Gamal Abdel Nasser. Shops in Ramallah were closed in mourning; school was dismissed for three days.

I wrote, "Everyone is quite upset. Nasser was the only Arab leader who championed the Palestinian cause. With him gone, nobody knows what their fate will be. It is truly a tragic time; Jordan is killing their relatives and friends, and now their one hope, Nasser, is gone."

Within that context, I can imagine why my letter to my mother included a request to tape a Johnny Mathis record and send it to me. "It is one of my favorites," I explained, "especially the 'Wonderful, Wonderful' song on the first side." The letter also had this comment: "We went to see 'Ben Hur' at the cinema last week. It was so interesting to see the Arabs cheering for a young Jewish boy. It was even more interesting to see their reaction to an Arab in the movie pinning the Star of David on Ben Hur when he drove the Arab's chariot!"

As life began returning to normal after the various crises of my first month in Ramallah—whatever "normal" is in the context of a military occupation—my letters home detailed the everyday challenges of school work, homesickness, unfamiliar foods, and the weather. Adjusting to a different culture and teaching classes I'd never taught before were weighing on me. "My evening preparations take up all my time, and I am really not enjoying it yet," I wrote in early October. "I get very despondent; there is nothing but my work, and when one's work is the problem, I'm in trouble! I didn't expect overseas work to be glamorous and romantic—and it surely is not!"

I missed American foods, although the girls school's cook who prepared supper for the foreign teachers each day tried to accommodate us. She even served tongue at my request! But I missed milk and was tired of the steady diet of "rice, eggplant, and other weird plants."

I was missing an Indiana fall and made a habit of taking a route between the boys school and girls school campuses that led me past the few trees in Ramallah that displayed a semblance of turning colors. The weather was getting chilly, and there was even an unseasonable early rain that coincided with Nasser's death. Occurring during a *khamisiyeh*, a meteorological phenomenon of winds blowing in off the North African desert, the iconic figure's death was met with rain that was mixed with red sand and dirt, a foreboding "raining blood" that many took as an omen.

I spent a great deal of time crying myself to sleep each night during those initial months. Sensing my misery, although I wouldn't admit it to others, my housemate Donn Hutchison would regularly come to my room around 9:00 p.m. with hot cocoa and fresh brownies, as I labored on schoolwork. It helped me make it through those rough months.

For all this adventure and depression, I was being paid a princely sum! "Since I have four years of college," I reported, "I get a pretty high salary: $84 a month. $40 of that goes for meals. Housing is free, so it really is adequate as long as I don't buy too many frills."

Further adding to the challenges of my first months in Palestine was a letter from Paula, the girlfriend I left behind in college. A mid-October letter of mine reported that she had developed a friendship with another man and needed to know whether I wanted to marry her or if she should get serious with this new relationship. I called her, proposed, and we began making plans for her to join me the next year to get married and teach at the girls school.

By early November, my letters indicated that I was beginning to settle into the routine of teaching. "School is going fine. I'm getting more and more accustomed to the classroom, but I'm not the disciplinarian the school wants. Oh well; I'll get gruff and mean with age. My math classes are more fun now, and English is almost a pleasure." I was also indicating, however, that I was already beginning to contemplate taking a different vocational course when I would return to the States.

My life in Ramallah was beginning to develop into a comfortable routine. Hard work teaching, preparing, and grading, Monday through Thursday, was punctuated by the Friday holiday. Saturday was another class day before we were off again for Sunday. Thursday evenings were often spent going to the cinema to see three-year-old films in English or hilarious Bollywood movies from India. My housemate and I would also visit friends in the local Quaker community to watch TV or play card games. Our joke about our exciting lives was that the highlight of our Thursday evening routine was pumping water from the cistern into the tank in our attic that fed our pipes by gravity.

Indeed, for the duration of my time in Ramallah, Swift House, the old mission home where I lived, was not on city water. All the water came from cisterns fed by the rains that fell in Palestine between November and April of each year. We had to boil any water we consumed, and our use of water had to be strictly limited. If we ran out before the rainy season, it was just tough luck. We took Quaker showers: get in, get wet, turn off the water, soap up, rinse off, and get out of there in two minutes!

Clothes were washed in an old wringer washer, our four loads weekly all going through the same water and not rinsed. They had to be shaken out rigorously to get the soapy residue off before hanging on outside lines in the blazing sun. Otherwise, they would dry almost instantly into whatever shape they were hung in. That water was then used to wash the floors. I often joked with guests that we then used the remaining water to cook.

Using rainwater meant that the tile roof of Swift House had to be cleaned each fall and the downspouts into the cisterns checked for leaks. My first fall in Ramallah, I was given that task, and as I swept pine needles and other detritus off the roof, I found shrapnel still there from the '67 war three years before. I learned later that Israeli bombardments had gone over Swift House but killed children in a neighboring house.

While I was becoming more comfortable in the classroom, I still struggled to keep up in the higher math courses. "I'm in sections in math now that completely floor me," I wrote in another November letter, "but I'll get along. The problem is that the math I am teaching here to 10th and 11th grade students is not offered to American students until 12th grade or college." I learned later from a math professor at Earlham College that the books we were using at the Friends School were experimental math texts that he had helped develop and were never intended to be used for high school students.

One of the ways I got along in math was depending on the brilliance of several of my students whose competency in the subject was far beyond mine. That and the occasional dream. On one occasion, I had assigned the problems in my calculus class for the next day, and as was my custom, worked them out that night to make sure I could do them. One problem stumped me, and I worked past midnight trying to solve it, to no avail. I finally went to bed, planning to get up early and give it another go when my mind was fresh.

Around 4:00 a.m., I awoke with a start, having dreamed the answer. I leapt out of bed and jotted down on a piece of paper what I had dreamed and then went back to sleep. Awaking at my usual hour, I dashed to my desk to see if I had actually solved the problem or only dreamed that I had found the answer. Indeed, there it was—the problem was worked out correctly. As I checked my dreamworks against my calculations from the night before, I recognized that I had been making the same minor arithmetical error over and over but had been too tired to see it. In my sleep, that part of my brain shut down, but the more integrative hemisphere kept whirring away at it until the problem was solved. I tried that technique in the graduate studies that came in succeeding years, but putting theology books under my pillow at night never worked the same.

The end of the first third of the school year coincided in 1970 with Thanksgiving in America. I reported that the school cook, Jelilia, would be fixing a turkey along with some of the traditional fixings. I lamented that "it just won't seem the same without oyster dressing and picking corn on the farm on a bright, crisp fall morning the way we used to." I also noted that Thanksgiving was not a traditional holiday in Palestine. "Arabs and Israelis didn't have a get-together in 1620." But the feast coincided that year with Ramadan, the Muslim month of fasting, so we would get two days out of school. Unfortunately, Thanksgiving was also attended by the news of the assassination in Cairo of the Jordanian prime minister, Wasfi Tal. Palestinians were not unhappy; they believed he was behind the Black September purge of the Palestine Liberation Organization from Jordan. Talk of war continued to spread, with people stocking up provisions. Calmer heads maintained it was unfounded fear and that any fighting would be near the Suez Canal.

Everyday conversation continued to be dominated by the realities of the military occupation, and anger still simmered over the expulsion of 750,000 Palestinians from their homes with the establishment of the state of Israel in 1948 and the subsequent war. The hymnals in the Friends meetinghouse had the word Israel blacked out in the hymn, "O Come O Come Emmanuel and Ransom Captive Israel." My students' English essays often included fanciful tales of their sneaking out of their homes at night to join the *fedayeen* fighters in Jordan and attack Israeli army installations. All hoped that the international community would intervene and end Israel's occupation of the West Bank and Gaza. There was no talk yet of an independent Palestinian state.

Following Thanksgiving, I made the decision to fly home for the long Christmas break. My quick engagement to Paula also turned out not to be dampening her growing relationship with someone else, and I flew home to try to figure things out. It turned into a depressing holiday, as we broke off the engagement. My family was upset, and I struggled to decide whether I should even return to Ramallah. My status with Selective Service and my pride won out, and I returned in time to face mid-term exams at the school, preparing six different exams and grading 216 tests.

Breaking up the depression of events back home and the tedium of grading mid-terms was the excitement of a Swift House haunting. For three nights in mid-January, my housemate Donn was visited by an apparition; the last night it even got into bed with him. This was no dream of the calculus variety; Donn was fully awake. The ghost was evidently selective in its visitation, however, never bothering to come to my bedroom.

Also bringing added excitement to the scene was growing tension in the Middle East. Egypt expressed an unwillingness to extend the ceasefire past early February, and many believed again that war was inevitable. My students were all for it; the Egyptian army seemed ready; about 500 Russian advisers were in Egypt; President Sadat said that if the people wanted war—and they appeared to—then they would have to accept the cost. The Egyptian people seemed to be ready. Some fighting continued in Jordan from the conflict in the fall, but Ramallah remained calm.

The calm extended well past the ceasefire deadline, the threats of war falling flat, as flat as a tire on an outing to the Dead Sea that I joined with three other expats that month. Just outside of Bethlehem, we got the spare tire out of the car, only to find it was flat, too. As two of us walked into Bethlehem with the tire to get it fixed, a bus picked us up and took us to a taxi that drove us on to town. The tire was repaired in no time, and meanwhile, back at the car, locals had brought tea to the two women who remained behind.

Completing the trip to the Dead Sea, we visited the mountain fortress of Masada, climbing to the top of the legendary site on the earthen ramp that Roman soldiers had built by slave labor over a two-year period in the early 70s C.E. to overcome more than 900 Jewish rebels. When the Roman army finally broke through the defenses, they found that all had committed suicide.

At that time, certain units of the Israel Defense Forces were sworn in on top of Masada as a symbolic expression of "Masada (and Israel) will not fall again!" Over the many succeeding visits to Masada that I made, I observed the expansion of the archaeological excavations, the improvement in amenities for tourists, and a striking change in the narrative, as Israel decided that the story of suicide was not a story the nation needed, and soldiers were no longer sworn in there.

Meanwhile, back in my love life, Paula was breaking things off with her other boyfriend but not yet sure what she wanted to do with our relationship. I was growing more confident in my teaching. I was beginning to settle in. A letter home in mid-February expressed it this way:

> By next year I hope to have my subjects mastered, my personal problems solved, and settle down to some serious teaching. This whole experience is sure to help me somehow. It looks like the U.S. is getting in deeper in Southeast Asia. Lands sakes, it just may well be safer here! Nobody knows what will happen when the new ceasefire ends in March. We're all pretty much confused about it. It doesn't help to read the Book of Joshua in the Bible, though, as I have been doing lately!

But just as I was settling in, I developed an intestinal problem that required hospitalization. After five days in a Palestinian hospital outside of Jerusalem, within sight of the Mount of Olives, a marvelous doctor, attentive French nuns as nurses, antibiotics, and some less-than-leisurely intestinal groping, I was good to go. The total cost of the hospital stay? $75. My Farm Bureau insurance from back home covered it all. Annual premiums? $24.

We had a visit that winter from Sok Hon Ham, a Quaker known in his homeland as the Korean Gandhi. A former minister of education in Korea, he had spent more than two years in prison for his ideas of peace.

Another winter of '71 visitor was Landrum Bolling, then president of Earlham College and primary author of the ground-breaking book *Search for Peace in the Middle East*. We didn't know it at the time, but he was engaged in secret diplomatic efforts for the United States in the Middle East. All we knew was that he had been visiting with leaders in Egypt, Israel, and Jordan—and even members of the Palestine Liberation Organization in Lebanon. Speaking in meeting for worship at the Ramallah Friends meetinghouse one Sunday, he shared how things seemed more hopeless than he'd ever seen them, but he said, we can never give up hope. Indeed, Landrum never did, continuing his peace work until his death at the age of 104 in 2018.

Another message in meeting for worship that I recall to this day was from Jean Zaru. She rose out of the silence to ask, "Should I serve the military governor my best chocolate cake?" As the wife of the principal of the boys school, she had been told that the Israeli military governor would be visiting, and she anticipated the demands on her as she hosted the delegation at their home in Grant Hall. She did, indeed, decide to serve her best cake, and years later she confided in me how the visit had gone.

Surrounded by his military guards, the commander began his conversation with a condescending remark about Palestinians. "You have such beautiful flowers around your home," he said. "I'm surprised. We Israelis love flowers. Arabs don't." He went on in many ways to emphasize the control Israel had over the area—and over the school. And Jean served them her best chocolate cake. When the visit concluded, and the military governor and his entourage left, Jean noticed that one of the guards had dropped his pistol on the couch. She followed the group outside, holding the gun by its barrel, and called to them, "Pardon me, but I think you left something." Jean said that the Israelis were as surprised by her gesture as by the presence of flowers in an Arab home.

I continued to do my own traveling as I tried to wrap my mind around the geography—both physical and political—of the region. On a trip to Hebron, I visited the city's famous glass blowers, viewed the oak under which Abraham presumably rested when he arrived in the area 4,000 years ago, and saw the tombs of Abraham, Sarah, and other patriarchs and matriarchs in the Ibrahimi Mosque. Another American teacher and I spent a day in Gaza, enjoying the beach, getting our car wheels buried in the sand and dug out by helpful locals, and purchasing a famed Gazan rug. Visits to Jerusalem took me to some of the holiest sites in Judaism, Christianity, and Islam: the Western Wall (*Kotel*), the Church of the Resurrection (Holy Sepulchre), and the Dome of the Rock and al-Aqsa Mosque.

On one visit to Jerusalem, I stopped by the Garden Tomb, an alternative location for the burial and resurrection of Jesus, maintained by an evangelical wing of the Anglican Church. Also in the garden at that time was a large group of American tourists who turned out to be members of Billy James Hargis's Christian Crusade against Communism organization. They were on a tour of "the last bastions against Communism"—Greece, Israel, Rhodesia, and South Africa. A few struck up a conversation with me and learning that I was from Indiana, excitedly told me that they knew for a fact that the stone for the third Jerusalem temple had been quarried in Bedford, Indiana, and was stored in a warehouse there, awaiting Christ's return. Since there was no shortage of limestone around Jerusalem I thought it might be less labor intensive simply to buy local.

Back at the school, as the students and I became more comfortable with each other, there was good-natured bantering between us. They were very well acquainted with the types of Israeli jets that constantly flew overhead. "That's a French Mirage," they would say as a plane roared past. "That's an Israeli Kfir." When another jet buzzed past, they would say, "That Phantom, Mr. Carter, is one of yours!"

The other news I continued to share in letters to my mother was about the ongoing drama with Paula. She finally broke up with her other boyfriend, applied again to teach at the girls school, and said she was coming over to get married. Having reconciled myself to the break-up, I was not overly convinced that this was a good idea. I went ahead with it, though, and plans were made for a summer wedding in Ramallah.

With that drama subsiding and no imminent fighting anticipated even after yet another ceasefire expired, the school year continued to go well, and I felt more and more confident in my teaching. I also felt more and more comfortable in Swift House. No more ghostly visitations, and the intense cold of a Palestinian winter was giving way to spring warmth. Trees were budding, and the valleys around the town were blanketed in a rainbow of Palestinian wildflowers. I relished them on hikes through the *wadis* (valleys), and I would have luxuriated in them even more had I known what would become of those areas in only a few short decades: filled with the ever-expanding construction in Ramallah and El-Bireh or confiscated by spreading Israeli settlements.

The extended Easter holiday of that spring also saw me grow the beard that I have kept ever since. Although I was continuing to grow in confidence in the classroom, I still felt a little intimidated by how much older some of my students looked than I did at twenty-two years of age. I grew the beard in self-defense. When I retired from teaching in 2015, I joked with my college students that one of the reasons I was ready to leave the profession was that I realized my beard was older than their parents.

As that first year of teaching wrapped up, I took on another task. The Friends meeting asked me to fill in as pastoral minister after my housemate, the former minister, had to go to the States to attend to an ill sister. I had even less preparation for that responsibility than I did for teaching. Fortunately, it meant only preaching and not any counseling or other pastoral duties. There were sufficient guest speakers to spare the congregation from my weekly sermons, and fortunately, Donn returned later in the year and resumed his previous service. The very first words spoken to me by Jirius Mansur, the meeting clerk, before my initial sermon were, "Don't protract the message too much. We don't want to be bored." My tenure as short-term pastor turned out OK, but the congregation was happy when other options presented themselves.

My wedding took place in the meetinghouse in June, with my mother and a brother attending, along with members of the meeting, fellow teachers, and students. After a half-day honeymoon at the YMCA in East Jerusalem, Paula and I entertained my family members on various outings to biblical sites before they returned to the States.

That first summer was spent participating in an American Friends Service Committee international work camp in Ramallah. Young people from the U.S., England, Finland, the Netherlands, and Germany joined twenty Arab youth in a project at the Boy Scouts Center. Israeli youth were supposed to join in, but that never happened, as we were told that none of the Palestinians would take part if there were Israelis in the camp.

Our work under a blazing sun and cloudless sky for two weeks involved repairing a stone wall to abate winter cave-ins, leveling land for an outdoor park, and preparing another piece of land for an athletic area for long jump, parallel bars, high jump, and pole vault. It was hard labor; we had to move ten dump truck loads of gravel along with all the earth moving. All was done with *quffas*, little rubber buckets made out of used tires. Even now they make me think of one of my students back then, Imanuel Quffa. Referring to the Hebrew meaning of his first name and the Arabic meaning of his surname, he jokingly referred to himself as "God with us . . . in a bucket!"

The AFSC work camp ended with the Americans in the camp preparing a typical meal for the group: ten roast chickens with dressing, five pans of corn bread, a big pot of green beans, and two deep dish apple cobblers. The food was great. Following the time in Ramallah, the group spent a week attending a seminar in Jerusalem. We heard from Israeli officials, including the press secretary for the Israel Defense Forces, as well as various Arab spokespeople, including a leader of the Palestinian Arab national movement. We also visited an Israeli kibbutz. All went well, although the Arab young people did not participate.

Meanwhile, matters in the Arab world were tense. There were two attempted coups in Sudan and Morocco, neither affecting life in Palestine much. But Jordan continued to mop-up the after-effects of Black September. They had practically eliminated any PLO presence in the kingdom. Some one hundred PLO fighters actually fled to Israel and surrendered, feeling safer in the hands of the enemy than they did in Jordan.

At summer's end, I looked forward to the new school year with a confidence I didn't have in my first year teaching. The drama of a long-distance relationship was over, and although no conversation was free of mention of the military occupation's impact, the political situation was calm. My teaching load was even going to be a bit lighter—one geometry course was given to a Palestinian teacher returning from the States, Sina Mansur. The daughter of the Friends meeting clerk, she had already won my affection by responding to her father's comment to me on my first day of bringing the prepared message. At Jirius's directive not to speak too long or be boring, Sina turned to me and said, "Don't pay any attention to him, Max. Don't let him bully you!" I liked her from the start.

We also welcomed three new American teachers and one administrator. John Voss and David and Mary Wilson would be teaching, and Anna Langston would assume the duties of principal of the girls school. They made for lively conversation and helped fill the void left by Liesel Dreisbach, who returned to the States after one year teaching at the girls school. David, especially, was intriguing. A former Catholic seminarian who had become a Quaker, he broadened my perspectives on scripture and church history—and told bawdy tales of life in a semi-cloistered, seminary setting.

He was also something of a psychic. During Mary and David's first visit to Swift House, David took a self-guided stroll around the old mission house and returned to the kitchen, where the rest of us were having tea. "Is this house haunted?" David asked. I told him about Donn's encounter with the apparition the previous year. "I thought so," he replied. "As I was coming down the stairs from looking around the second floor, a ghost passed through me ascending the stairway."

One problem did hover over the opening of school that August: President Nixon's economic "Great Leap Forward" had caused turmoil in international currency. The Israeli pound was devalued by twenty percent, causing prices to skyrocket, and teachers were worried about how their salaries would be adjusted to compensate for it. As it turned out, those adjustments were made.

My letters home that fall also indicated that I had adjusted to teaching. "School has started, and it is a whole lot more fun this year than last. I teach 26 hours instead of 29, and discipline in the classroom is better. The new teachers are struggling with the same problems with students I had last year. I guess it wasn't just me after all."

Early in the new school year, around the Muslim holiday of Eid ul-Miraj, I related this exchange with my students: I asked them what the festival signified, and one Muslim student explained that it marked the time when the Prophet Muhammad was carried by his steed to "the farthest mosque," traditionally believed to be the site of the al-Aqsa Mosque in Jerusalem, where he ascended into the heavens and communed with the prophets.

With that, one of the Christian students blurted out, "Yeah, sure! A horse sprouts wings and flies Muhammad around! You expect us to believe that?!" Without hesitation, the Muslim student responded, "And Jesus walked on water?"

It was an innocent enough exchange among good friends, but it got me thinking about how we take for granted the unbelievable in our own religious traditions and view with skepticism the similarly miraculous in others' religions.

Though in my classroom differences led to good-natured bantering, matters were not as civil in the wider region. While it was calm in the occupied territories, the Suez Canal front was erupting in hostilities. An Egyptian and an Israeli plane had been shot down. Jordanians and Palestinians were deadlocked in their post-Black September negotiations, and a "brash young leader in Libya, Gadaffi, was injured in a car accident." I reported that Israel was upset about a debate at the United Nations over the status of Jerusalem, and the Arab states were upset about Israel's actions in the holy city. "Ted Kennedy was in Israel last week and made all the same comments that all other presidential hopefuls make about Israel: increase arms shipments and support Israel's occupation of the territories."

There continued to be problems with the devaluation of Israeli currency, wiping out teacher raises. My $83 monthly salary and my wife's $59 monthly compensation made it a challenge to cover our expenses, and we were eating one meal a day. But at least the cisterns still had water in them ahead of the coming rainy season.

I continued to enjoy the company of the new teachers at the school, and we even traveled to West Jerusalem together. Visiting the home of Frank and Pat Hunt, American Friends Service Committee staff assigned to Palestine and Israel, we had a supper with them that had been prepared by their Palestinian cook. In typical form, the cook insisted that we have seconds and kept encouraging us to eat more. As she urged the Hunts' young boy, Timothy, to take more fish, he struggled to communicate to her in Arabic that he had had enough. He knew the word for "enough" (*bikafi*), but he didn't know the word for "fish" (*samak*). Gesturing to the cook, he kept saying "Fish bikafi; fish bikafi!" as she continued to pile on the food. In Arabic, *fish bikafi* means "not enough!"

The other news from the fall was that I had decided to apply for admission to the Earlham School of Religion (ESR) upon returning to the States, rather than continue my plan of applying for high school teaching positions. My experience of teaching had convinced me that the joys of the high school classroom were overrated, but more importantly, I had come to a growing conviction that my vocation ought to harmonize with my passions, and as I reflected on what my passion had been as an undergraduate, I realized that it had not been in my academic studies in German and math as much as it had been in my involvement in the campus ministry program of the Ball State Fellowship of Friends under the guidance of Quaker saint Ruth Day.

That awareness came home to me one night as we returned from a monthly meeting of the Mennonite, Brethren, and Quaker volunteers working in various programs in Palestine and Israel. I had been impressed by the others' experience of community in their collegiate studies at denominational campuses and yearned for that same sense of community and vocational calling. Feeling more and more that my vocation was in the kind of ministry that had been so important to me at Ball State, I was flipping through a copy of *Quaker Life* magazine that evening back at Swift House when I came across an advertisement from ESR. It announced a new program—a concentration in preparation for campus ministry. That night I determined to apply.

By mid-October of that second year, however, I wrote home that the "bubble of exuberance" I had been feeling with my teaching and my decision to apply to ESR had burst. I reported on a visit by us American teachers to the principal of the boys school to express our concern about physical discipline of students. It was against school policy and our own sense of Quaker pedagogy to use corporal punishment on students, yet we regularly witnessed the slapping of students and other physical punishment.

To put it mildly, our concerns were not met with great sympathy. In fact, our visit to the principal's home and confrontation about the disciplinary issue was seen as a major breach of hospitality. It caused great tension for some time thereafter, even affecting the Friends meeting where we attended. I expressed my eagerness to be done with the apparent lack of application of Quaker principles in education and to begin my studies at ESR.

Tensions were also continuing to be felt in the region. "The Arabs are getting stronger," I wrote in the same letter, "which is having the effect of forcing Israel into demanding more arms from the U.S. I hear that the Senate has voted overwhelmingly to ship more arms." In a conversation with an American Jewish tourist in West Jerusalem one time, I mentioned that I had heard from some in Israel that the answer to their security fears was to become the 51st state in the U.S. "Oh, no," the person replied, only half jokingly, "then we'd have only two senators. Now we have one hundred!"

I continued in the letter by saying that we also were experiencing great excitement at Swift House: "We are rearranging the furniture, putting the winter rugs down, and painting the windows above the fireplace red, blue, and yellow."

Another letter, later in October, mentioned the added excitement of our American group's evening at Sina Mansur's apartment, listening to the album of *Jesus Christ, Superstar*. It had yet to be made into a movie, so this was the original Broadway soundtrack. The next year back in the States, when the movie version came out, I was delighted to see that the opening scene had the cast arriving on the outdoor set in the familiar red and white Ramallah/Jerusalem bus that I had ridden on many times.

A constant theme in letters home was also my yearning for familiar American food. A chance to fix mac and cheese was cause for excitement. For my birthday that fall, I was thrown a supper party featuring fried chicken, mashed potatoes and gravy, salad, dinner rolls, and cherry delight for dessert. I was a happy boy.

On my birthday, I also received a six-week old puppy that I named *Shatra*, the Arabic for "clever." She was an absolute delight and brightened our home for several months before she was killed by a taxi while she attempted to run across the road between Swift House and the boys school. It was devastating, and we buried her lovingly in the yard where the school's *Kaykab* garden is now.

Another late birthday present was acknowledgment that our differences with the boys school principal over discipline had been worked out and that all hurt feelings had been smoothed over.

Also enabling the year to proceed more easily was my short-lived tenure as the interim pastor of the Ramallah Friends Meeting. When a theologically-trained Mennonite, Rachel Friesen, arrived with her family to work with the Mennonite Central Committee programs in Palestine, she agreed to assume the duties. I was greatly relieved.

We continued to be graced with interesting visitors in worship at the meeting, typically tourists or volunteers and professional staff with religious organizations or NGOs. One local, though, who was a regular visitor was an Israeli Jew, Yusuf Abileah. A violinist with the Haifa symphony and early kibbutznik well before the establishment of the state of Israel, he began attending the Friends meeting when the borders opened after the '67 war. A pacifist, he enjoyed the association with fellow travelers.

One story I recall him telling was of working in the fields during the 1929 Arab Revolt. On a Friday after the noon prayers in the mosque of the Arab village neighboring his kibbutz, he found himself surrounded by a group from the village. "We're sorry," a leader of the group said, "but we have to kill you." Yusuf asked them why, and they responded that the imam of the mosque had preached on how the kibbutzniks were part of an organized plot to steal the Arabs' land and that they must be killed.

"Well, I'm sorry about that," Yusuf told them. "I don't want to be killed. What can we do about this?" "We like you and don't want to kill you either," the leader responded. "But if you convert to Islam, we wouldn't have to!" "How do I do that?" Yusuf replied. "You simply have to say that there is no god but the one God and that Mohammad is a prophet of

God." "I can do that," Yusuf said. He repeated the Muslim statement of faith, the *shahada*, and the villagers heaved a sigh of relief and returned to their homes.

My letters home shared news about the weather, reports that school continued to go well, that I had decided not to fast with Muslims during Ramadan, shopping trips to West Jerusalem, and assurances that the talk of impending war and army mobilizations was just that—talk. I delighted in the upcoming Christmas vacation which, because of Latin and Orthodox observances, would last from December 23 to January 10, followed by a five-day Muslim holiday and then a week off for mid-term exams. It felt like it was almost February, and I was barely into December.

As we entered the Christmas break, we learned that Israel had extended the city limits of Jerusalem to within a mile of where we lived in Ramallah, very near the traditional site of the biblical judge Deborah's home. I joked that when I first went to Ramallah, I lived nine miles from Jerusalem, and by my second year, I lived one mile from the city—and I hadn't moved.

The major excitement beyond the many vacation days was an encounter I had with the Israeli police. In late January I was informed that my tourist visa had expired and that I would have to leave the country immediately. I had a meeting with the police commander in the station near the boys school, told them that I couldn't leave at that time, leaving my students and the school in the lurch, and requested to see the military governor. My request was granted.

Accompanied by Fuad Zaru, the principal of the boys school, I went to see the Israeli commander of the occupied West Bank in his office in the British Mandate era military fortress in Ramallah. It was an imposing edifice, and the officer was an imposing figure. Rising from behind his desk as I entered his office, he said, "Ah, Mr. Carter! I've been following your case with great interest. I'm going to let you stay. Israel hasn't received its latest shipment of Phantom jets from the U.S., and I don't want to jeopardize it!"

And so, I remained the rest of the school year without any trouble—other than my troubled conscience at having been partially responsible for yet another shipment of armaments into the region.

As school resumed following the long break, I received the tragic news from home that a high school classmate of mine, Lita Hallam, had died shortly after the birth of her baby. She had dated one of my brothers and one of my best friends, and we had been in the school's production of *Our Town* together our senior year. She played the role of Emily, whose death in the play eerily paralleled Lita's. As my English class resumed that winter, our first reading assignment was Thornton Wilder's *Our Town*.

The political situation continued to keep us alert even while things were calm around Ramallah. Israel made a four-day incursion into southern Lebanon, and talk was spreading that Jordan's King Hussein and Israel were close to making an agreement about returning the West Bank to Jordan. Nobody in the Palestinian community, however, had been consulted.

At the end of March, several of us from the Ramallah Friends Meeting made the trip to Lebanon to attend Near East Yearly Meeting of Friends at the Quaker school in Brummana. We had to go by way of Cyprus, however, since passports with an Israeli stamp in them would prevent us from entering Lebanon. We obtained new U.S. passports at the American embassy in Cyprus and enjoyed our brief stay in Nicosia, purchasing Cypriot lace and viewing the dividing lines between the Turkish and Greek areas.

As we arrived in Beirut and went through passport control at the airport, the agent looked at my fresh, new passport, winked, and said, "So, how are things down South?" I said that I wasn't from the South; I was from Indiana. He smiled knowingly, nodded his head in the direction of Lebanon's southern border, and said, "No, I mean down South—in Israel! How are things there?" I said they were fine; he laughed; we moved on.

After nearly two years living under a military occupation in the West Bank, I felt like I could breathe freely in Lebanon. It was a feeling that is hard to explain, but it was liberating. The sessions of the yearly meeting were enjoyable, even though there was some tension over how to express Quaker concern on the continuing Israeli occupation of the Sinai, Golan Heights, Gaza, and the West Bank. Not all was Quaker business, though. We took a tour of the Beka'a Valley, including the famous Roman temple of Bacchus and remains of a temple dedicated to Jupiter; we visited the ancient city of Byblos and took a boat out into the Mediterranean from the same port used by the Phoenicians. The people we met among Friends in Lebanon were also very interesting: a poet-architect who was developing a new Arabic alphabet; the co-founder of the Mideast's largest cannery; an influential medical doctor; and the woman who taught Lawrence of Arabia his Arabic.

Back in Ramallah, we were greeted by the joyous news of the birth of the Wilsons' baby girl on April 13. She was named Erika Nissan (*Nissan* being Arabic for the month of April) and kept us entertained the rest of the school year. When we other American teachers went into Jerusalem to visit the Wilsons in the hospital the first time, we jokingly sang the Simon and Garfunkel song that was popular at the time, "All Gone to Look for America," substituting *Im-Erika* for America—the Arabic expression for "mother of Erika."

As the school year continued into its final weeks that spring, the big excitement in town was that municipal elections would be held the first week in May, the first elections since the military occupation of 1967. The town was plastered with candidate posters and banners.

Visits from international Friends continued, especially as some came on to Palestine from the yearly meeting sessions in Lebanon. I was especially intrigued by the visit of Hannah and Christopher Taylor, British Friends representing the Friends World Committee for Consultation. They also represented an interesting bit of Quaker business history in England. Hannah was a Cadbury, and Christopher was a retired executive with the old Quaker chocolate company.

Final trips throughout the region were also crammed into the remaining weeks of my time in Ramallah. We toured the religious sites around the Sea of Galilee, the new Church of the Annunciation in Nazareth, the Baha'i temple in Haifa, and the coastal cities of Netaniya and Tel Aviv.

As we began packing our things for shipping back home and planning our trip through Europe to the States, we learned the happy news that Donn Hutchison and Sina Mansur were engaged. They would go on to marry the following year and have two children before Sina contracted breast cancer and died in her mid-30s. Donn raised the children in Swift House as he continued to teach at the Friends Boys School.

In early June I finished my teaching in Ramallah with six final exams to type up, forty-six term papers to grade, forty-nine end-of-semester tests, and twenty-three book reports. An endless round of final visits, teachers' meetings, and a student/teacher party in Jericho were crammed into the busy end of the school year. Still, three of us American teachers found time to visit two British Quakers working in Gaza. It was a time not only for relaxing on the sand and swimming in the Mediterranean but also of witnessing the terrible contrast between the beauty of the beach and the grinding poverty of the refugee camps. At that time, 360,000 people were crammed into the six miles wide by twenty-fve miles long stretch of the Strip. Nearly all of those people were located in ten camps and a few small towns. The majority of the land was in citrus groves and vineyards, with forty percent of the Strip as waste land. The population density was 3,100 per square mile. The Netherlands, by contrast, the most densely populated country on earth at the time, had 850 people per square mile.

When I left Palestine that summer, I had no thought about returning; I was happy to be heading into a new chapter in my life, having fulfilled my alternative service requirement. But my great-aunt Annice's other statement to me in August of 1970 as she saw me off at the airport proved prophetic. After telling me to be careful of the Carter reputation in Ramallah, she told me, "Max, if you stay two years in Ramallah, you will always go back." She was right.

Annice Carter (left) with some Friends Girls School boarding students on an excursion to the Dead Sea in the late 1950s.

With some of my students at the Friends Boys School in 1972. Front, left to right: Imanuel (Hanna) Quffa, Fawaz Afranji, myself, Ghassan Ayoub, Salah Abdu Jaleel. Back: Ghassan Abdo and Zuhdi Dajani. Among them are professors, a chemist, an engineer, a physician, and a computer expert. I evidently did them minimal harm.

Annice Carter wearing a traditional Palestinian thobe. They are intricately cross-stitched in patterns and colors unique to particular villages and regions. Annice's thobe is readily identified as from Ramallah.

Jean Zaru in the front garden of the Friends Boys School.

Swift House, built in the early 1900s as the mission house for the schools.

Pillars of the Ramallah Friends Meeting, Ellen and Jirius Mansur.

Site of the destroyed Palestinian village of Imwas, biblical Emmaus. It was razed by Israel following the '67 War, and a national park was established in its place. A taxi driver pointed it out to me as he drove me from the Tel Aviv airport to Ramallah.

Chapter 2: Occasional Activity

Annice Carter's prediction did not come true for several years. My then-wife and I returned to the States by way of Europe, heeding the advice of some seasoned workers in the Middle East to spend time in Vienna first, as it was a "half-way" spot between the pace of the East and that of the West. Indeed, we needed the adjustment from the disorienting experience of living under military occupation in a different culture to resuming a "normal" life in the West.

While the time in Ramallah certainly affected me in many ways, I mostly put it out of my mind as we settled into life in Muncie, Indiana, and resumed education for the two of us. I commuted to Richmond and the Earlham School of Religion, and Paula continued her studies at Ball State University. It wasn't long, though, before normal proved to be anything but. Paula and I separated the spring of '73, and we divorced later that year.

I moved to Richmond and took up residence at the Earlham School of Religion before assuming a position at Earlham College in the fall as the head resident of Bundy Hall, a men's residence hall. That position was part of an internship I was serving for my campus ministry concentration, the other part being working with campus minister at-large, Tom Mullen. It was through that work that I met Jane Deichler, an Earlham undergrad, in October of '73. We married in 1974.

But before meeting Jane, I took a trip to Pennsylvania to attend the wedding of Liesel Dreisbach, my teaching companion in Ramallah 1970/71. Accompanying me was Jennifer Hunt, new student at Earlham and daughter of the AFSC representatives in Jerusalem during my time in Palestine. While at the wedding we learned of the outbreak of the October War between Israel and the forces of Egypt and Syria. The festivities were interrupted by our deep concern for our friends in the region, and we followed the unfolding events throughout the weekend and in the car ride back to Indiana.

The continuing conflict was, of course, a topic of great concern on the Earlham College campus, too. Several of us at Earlham had experience in the Middle East, and the student body included those with personal ties to the various parties in the conflict. One of my Jewish residents left to go to Israel in support of the war effort.

As the war continued and was followed by a ceasefire, many students joined in late-night conversations about the situation as they gathered in my residence hall apartment. Some, like my Jewish student and I, had personal experience in the region. Many others were trying to understand the Middle East for the first time.

Misty Gerner was a first-year student who eventually double-majored in Peace & Conflict Studies and Religion at Earlham. With little knowledge about the Middle East but intense curiosity, she joined in the living room discussions in my apartment. She was one of what often-times were nearly two dozen students crowded into the room. The conversations were free-wheeling and intense, but Misty remained mostly quiet, just soaking it in.

After Earlham, Misty went on to do graduate work in political science at Northwestern University. When it came time to choose a topic for her Ph.D. dissertation, she recalled those dorm discussions and hearing for the first time a description of Palestinians that defied the dominant narrative that they were terrorists, an image hard to counteract after the 1972 Munich Olympics massacre of Israeli athletes by the Palestinian Black September group. Misty decided to research the Israeli-Palestinian conflict.

The result of her work was the 1991 book *One Land, Two Peoples: The Conflict over Palestine*. It became a much-used text in classrooms, and Misty developed an international reputation as a scholar in the area of the politics of the Middle East and a professorship at the University of Kansas. She became a mentor to countless students and a friend and mentor at a distance to our own daughter, Maia, who also went on to become a professor of Middle East politics and author of several books on the subject of Israel and Palestine.

My studies at ESR and work supervising 180 college men in the dorm kept me busy enough that there was little time to think about the Middle East beyond the war. In my Bible classes at the seminary, I did have occasion to share insights from my time in biblical locations, and I sometimes had opportunity to share in conversation about my perspective on the ongoing response in the international community to the '67 and '73 wars.

From time to time I was invited to share with Quaker groups about my experience in Ramallah, and they were typically more open to my descriptions of the situation involving Israel and the Palestinians—especially those who had previously heard my Great-Aunt Annice speak. One of my first outings to talk about my time at the Friends Boys School was with the United Society of Friends Women (USFW) group in Plainfield, Indiana, with Annice in the audience.

After my talk, I was relieved to get what passed for approval from her. She told me that I hadn't made any major mistakes and that I had actually shared appropriately and accurately about the situation. Annice was usually less political in her presentations to groups about her time in Palestine, focusing mostly on the missionary aspect of her work. But she could be pointed when confronted about her own sympathy for the Palestinians. When she got the usual, "But God gave the land to the Jews," her terse rejoinder was always, "It came with conditions!"

Shortly after I began my work at Earlham, I learned what Landrum Bolling had been doing when he dropped by to worship with Friends in Ramallah. Landrum had retired from the presidency of Earlham in 1973 but had maintained a home outside of Richmond. He often had students house-sit for him. One such student wandered into his office and found papers on Landrum's desk that detailed his secret shuttle diplomacy in the Middle East for the U.S. government. The student went to the media with the information—and he became *persona non grata* on campus. He later left Earlham, wrote his autobiography at age twenty-three, completed his education elsewhere, and attempted to run for Congress while still in his early twenties.

Following the '73 war, the next major event that engaged me with my experience in Palestine was the December '77 arrest in Tel Aviv of one of my former students in Ramallah, Sami Esmail. He was returning to Palestine from his studies in engineering at Michigan State University to attend to his dying father. Coming off the plane, he was taken into custody by Israeli officials and accused of belonging to an extremist Palestinian group and having attended a terrorist training camp. All were false accusations, but it resulted in his imprisonment, during which his father died without Sami's being able to visit him.

A national campaign was begun to free Sami, and I was able to speak on his behalf on campus, describing the Sami I knew—one of the math students I turned to on a regular basis to bail me out when I had no clue in calculus class. It was a great joy to learn of his release later in '78, and I was able to bring him to Earlham to talk about his experience.

In 1979, Jane and I were asked by Friends United Meeting to lead a work camp to the Friends Schools in Ramallah, and we worked on planning the trip with the help of first-year Earlham student Saleem Zaru, son of Fuad and Jean Zaru of the Friends Boys School and Ramallah Friends Meeting. The two-week return to the West Bank was accompanied by a group of Quakers ranging in age from ten months (our youngest daughter Lissa) to retirement age. One of the younger set was Lynn Peery, who remained to teach for two years at the girls school. One of the older set was Great-Aunt Annice, recruited by FUM to act as our cook and (one assumes) overseer of her grand-nephew.

Maia (3 1/2 yrs.) in front of Jane and Lissa (10 mos.) in front of me at the entrance to the Ramallah Friends meetinghouse in 1979.

The primary focus of the trip was work: the group made curtains for the assembly hall at the girls school and painted the playground equipment. But we also had opportunities to learn about the situation—both ancient and modern—in outings to the Galilee, Hebron, Jerusalem, and to the Israel Museum and Yad Vashem, the Holocaust museum. We also met with Jim and Debbie Fine, AFSC staff who operated a legal aid center in Jerusalem for Palestinians affected by the occupation. Through all of our trips through the West Bank, we witnessed the first construction of Israeli settlements in the occupied territories in the wake of the conservative Likud Party's accession to power in the Israeli government.

On our trip to Hebron, I was shocked to see the construction of Israeli settlements in the occupied West Bank. This is some of the first construction in Kiryat Arba.

One of the impressions during the trip that hit me hardest was the grim pessimism expressed by our Palestinian friends. With the Egypt/Israel peace treaty of March of '79, their major advocate in the region had retreated. They saw the occupation hardening, and Israel was making attempts to fully integrate its commercial systems into the territories. Israel had reacted harshly to any attempt by the Palestinians to organize themselves and had tried to install puppet leaders in various municipalities. One of the people who was attempting to express Palestinian leadership was the mayor of Ramallah, Karim Khalaf. We met with him in his office, and he described the challenges of promoting Palestinian autonomy under a military occupation. The next year, he lost his legs in a car bomb assassination attempt planned by an Israeli underground organization. In 1982 he was removed from office by Israel.

I was saddened to sense this pessimism and the growing atmosphere of despair, a grimness matched by the trash-filled streets and graffiti-covered walls and buildings. I was also sad to see that most of the students I had taught were no longer in Ramallah. The majority had left for education and work in Europe, England, the Gulf states, and the United States. I wondered whether I'd had a hand in educating the bright hope for the future of Palestine to leave.

One bright spot in the experience, though, was interaction with Annice. Having grown up almost in fear of her towering presence and stern demeanor as she took it upon herself to keep her grand-nephews and -nieces in line, I was delighted to witness the affection the people of Ramallah had for her and her kindnesses to our group.

Annice's trip with us marked her fiftieth year since first arriving in Palestine to teach home economics at the girls school. During her service in Ramallah, she became the principal of the girls school, retiring in 1965 after fourteen years of work over several decades. Many remembered her quiet financial support of poor students and her steady hand at guiding the school through difficult times.

But perhaps her most famous moment came in 1967, when FUM called Annice out of retirement to help orient the new principal of the girls school, Peggy Paull, after everything was turned topsy-turvy with the '67 war and Israel's occupation of the West Bank. Annice spent several months that summer and fall helping Peggy and the school adjust to the new circumstances. One night, as Annice was getting ready for bed, she heard a commotion in the courtyard of the girls school, and clad in her nightgown, went to the railing of the third-floor porch outside of her apartment. Peering into the darkness, she saw a jeep full of Israeli soldiers firing their guns into the tree tops, a typical activity following the occupation in an attempt to show the Palestinians who was in control.

"What are you doing down there?" Annice yelled.

"We're firing our guns into the trees, can't you see that?" came the response.

"I know that! Now stop it! You are scaring our girls. Turn that jeep around and leave here immediately—and close the gate behind you!"

Cowed by Annice as much as we grand-nephews and -nieces often were, the soldiers obliged, drove the jeep through the open gate, closed it behind them, and did not return.

Years later, I asked my friend Donn Hutchison, who knew Annice in those years in Ramallah, if she had ever told him about the event. He said she had, indeed, but had admitted that her knees were knocking under her nightgown.

Also contrary to the image I had of Annice was her loving care of our group when they got sick. In addition to buying the ingredients and preparing our daily meals, she attended with her homemade chicken noodle soup to those who fell ill from an unfortunate outing to a local restaurant. She had even brought her own noodles with her from Indiana. One of those she nursed back to health was Jane. All our relationships were changed from that moment on. It also proved to be the last time Annice was in her beloved Palestine.

Returning from Palestine that summer, I had a renewed interest in the Israeli-Palestinian situation and spoke and wrote more about it on campus in my new role as campus ministry coordinator. My views were not always met with approval. However, there was another strong voice at Earlham for understanding the Palestinian perspective. Anthony Bing, a professor of English literature, one-time dean of students, and head of the Peace & Conflict Studies program at Earlham, had studied in Lebanon and took student groups there. In 1982, he initiated a study abroad program in Jerusalem that spent a semester immersed in the situation.

In 1982, shortly before leaving Earlham to begin doctoral work at Temple University, I wrote an essay for the campus ministry newsletter that expressed some of the controversy over Israeli-Palestinian issues on campus:

> No issues of the campus ministry newsletter have elicited such response as those of the past two weeks. When the interfaith council decided to address the conflict in the Middle East, we did a two-part series, one week's edition looking at the conflict from a Palestinian

perspective and the next from an Israeli point-of-view. . . .

There were numerous responses to the writers, editors, and me, underscoring the complexity of a problem such as the Middle East, a conflict involving a mix of social, political, and religious concerns. . . . Feelings on the Middle East are intricately interwoven. I was made quite aware of this during the two years I lived there while teaching at the Quaker schools in Ramallah. On one occasion during a visit by my mother, we were in the home of one of my students, and the inevitable question was asked:

"Mrs. Carter, what do you think of our land?"

I didn't have time to send frantic signals that this was a loaded question, so mother proceeded to answer as any Hoosier farmer born and bred probably would:

"It has been a lovely week, and I've enjoyed all the sights, but the land is so rocky and barren; why would anyone want to fight over it?"

Luckily, the parents of my student displayed the typical Palestinian hospitality, and all was forgiven, but it was clear that to them the land was far more than rocks and barren hillsides. Even though it would never raise a good Indiana crop of corn, it was the land of their ancestors, of their national aspirations, and of the prophets of their religion.

Whether the issue is the Middle East, the Falkland Islands, nuclear disarmament, or anything else, there are always those saying, "Why would anyone make a fuss over that concern?" We need to remember that what may appear to us as barren—be it landscape, thinking, or action—may to another be fraught with meaning.

In the summer of 1982, Jane and I moved with our three young children to Philadelphia, where I began doctoral studies in American Religious History at Temple University. Intense studies and part-time teaching at Friends Select School occupied my time and attention, but Israel's invasion of Lebanon drew me into further concern for the Middle East.

The war in Lebanon coincided with my taking a course on the Holocaust with the ostensible "dean of Holocaust studies" in the United States, Franklin Littell. Having made his reputation as a scholar of Protestant studies early in his career, Littell moved into studying the Holocaust and the Christian involvement in and response to it. He organized annual Holocaust conferences and was one of the driving forces behind the movement to build a Holocaust museum in Washington, D.C. He counted among his personal friends such leading figures in the Jewish community as Robert Maxwell, Vidal Sassoon, and even Israeli Prime Minister Menachem Begin.

I was taking his course not only out of my own interest in broadening my perspectives but also because he would be my primary academic adviser for my work in American Religious History. I took every course he offered during my time at Temple.

Early in the course that fall, Franklin invited the class to his home in Philadelphia. Being unfamiliar with the city, I left early from home to make sure I found the address in time. I wound up being the first to arrive, and I was welcomed into the Littell home warmly. Franklin asked about me, and when he learned that I had just come from Earlham, he launched into a blistering critique of Landrum Bolling, his work in the Middle East, and his authorship of *Search for Peace in the Middle East*. He went on to say he had recently been in Israel, had met with Menachem Begin, and had even toured the Israeli-occupied parts of Lebanon. He spoke glowingly of Begin, Ariel Sharon, and the Israeli army's efforts there.

I swallowed hard, remembered that this professor held my life in his hands as my primary adviser, and proceeded against all logic to inform him that I had spent two years teaching in Palestine and had been there as recently as 1979. Franklin immediately changed the subject.

A few weeks into the Holocaust course, the Phalangist-led massacres in the Sabra and Shatila refugee camps in Lebanon occurred, and I chose to do my course research paper on Holocaust and genocide motifs in those massacres. Israel was implicated in the massacres because the Phalangists were their allies. Israeli commander Ariel Sharon was censured for his oversight—in both senses of the word. It felt like I was risking my academic future at Temple by choosing the topic, but I decided I could do no other.

Surprisingly, when I told Franklin Littell of my choice, he did not discourage me. Instead he gave me some suggestions for background reading and approved the topic. I spent the rest of the course reading the daily accounts of the Lebanon war and the inquiries into the massacre in every spare moment I had. The final paper reflected the growing national understanding that the massacre occurred with the awareness of the Israeli army and belief that Sharon had not acted appropriately in his delayed response. I stopped short of comparing the tragedy to the Holocaust but noted genocidal motifs and other themes that we had studied in the course. I received an "A-" for the paper, and I heaved the first of many sighs of relief in my work at Temple, though Franklin and I never again spoke directly about the Israeli-Palestinian conflict.

To put bread on the table while I was taking a full course load, Jane took in children at our house as an informal day care, and I taught part-time for the first two years at Friends Select School and then full-time for six years at Friends' Central School. I revived my dusty competency in geometry to teach that subject at both schools along with Bible, Quakerism, and world religions. I joked that the combination of religion and geometry was appropriate: it was "sacred space!"

Out of my interest in the Israeli-Palestinian situation and Quaker involvement in the region, I incorporated some attention to the topic in my religion courses. It was not without controversy, even though I attempted to be balanced in my presentation. I knew it was risky business, given my experience at Earlham and my awareness of the fact that the majority of my students were Jewish.

The high Jewish population in Quaker schools was a result of the background of the Jewish immigrants from Europe who settled in Philadelphia. Products of the Enlightenment, most of the Jews who arrived in the City of Brotherly Love in the 19th century were interested in assimilating, becoming Americans, and seeing their children become fully American. They did not start a private Jewish school system but enrolled their children in public schools.

In the mid-1900s, Jewish families who wanted a quality education for their children considered the alternatives to public schools. Catholic and Episcopal schools were out of the question, owing to the prominent display of Christian symbols and required Christian worship. Quaker schools, however, were an attractive possibility: no Christian symbols, and worship was sitting in silence for an hour once a week. Even the courses in Quakerism and Bible required in some schools was not off-putting to most families. As I was told on more than one occasion by the parents of my Jewish students, "We haven't done a good job of educating our children religiously; we're glad they are getting some religious education somewhere."

It didn't mean that there weren't some concerns in the Jewish community about how many of their youth were attending Quaker schools. One time while jogging the trail along Wissahickon Creek, I struck up a conversation with a fellow runner. When he learned that I was teaching at Friends' Central, he said quite earnestly, "I am a rabbi, and I am very worried about how many Jewish boys and girls are at Friends schools. What happens if they buy into Quaker pacifism? Will they be able to come to Israel's defense if attacked?"

I don't think the rabbi needed to worry. I was careful to have both Israeli and Palestinian perspectives presented, sometimes by Israelis and Palestinians themselves. I knew that there would be blowback any time the Palestinian experience was expressed in one of my courses. At Friends Select, one student, with the assistance of his parents, did everything in his power to subvert my teaching, both by his behavior in class and in complaints to the school's administration. When I confronted the student about his attitude, he readily admitted that his obstinate behavior was intentional and directly related to my perceived sympathy for Palestinians.

At Friends' Central, each time the topic was raised in a class, I could expect to be called to the office of the school head following a visit by a representative of the Philadelphia Jewish Federation. One time I wound up in the waiting room outside the office with the Federation staff member. I asked him what the Federation's concern was, given that I had presented both Israeli and Palestinian perspectives. He maintained that too much legitimacy had been given to the Palestinian side and that the Israeli narrative had not been argued sufficiently. In other words, I was supposed to have argued that only the Israeli position was valid.

I decided to ask him how he would feel if he were in a Palestinian's position living under military occupation. "How would you act as a young person in that situation?" I asked. I was surprised by his candid answer: "I would join the armed resistance to that occupation," he said.

It didn't stop the regular visits from the Federation, but to their credit, the administration of both Friends Select and Friends' Central supported me in my continuing to introduce the subject in my religion classes. They admonished me only to try to maintain a balance. Personally, I felt that "balance" in an asymmetrical situation of oppression favored the oppressor, but I tried.

I once asked a Philadelphia rabbi to help me understand the apparently unquestioning support for Israel's treatment of the Palestinians, given the progressive attitude of the Jewish community on most other issues of human rights and justice. "You'll never understand it," he told me, "until you realize that many liberal American Jews do not believe in God and don't have a conventional religious faith. In the place of a deity and orthodox religion, they have Israel. To question Israel is the equivalent of attacking a person's belief in God or their religious faith."

The time in Philadelphia not only challenged me in the ways some responded to my advocacy for a just peace in the Middle East, it also broadened and deepened my understanding of Judaism, Islam, and even Christianity. My courses at Temple included exposure to two of the leading authorities on Islam in the world: Ismail al-Faruqi and Seyyed Hossein Nasr. I studied Judaism with two other noted authorities: Rabbis Arthur Waskow and Zalman Schachter-Shalomi. I visited mosques, synagogues, and temples with my high school classes. I also became involved with the Quaker/Jewish dialogue group in Philadelphia, a group that spent a full year getting to know each other socially before delving into the tricky business of Israel and Palestine.

Friends Girls School, showing the porch where Annice Carter stood in her confrontation with soldiers

Evocative sculpture on the grounds of Yad Vashem, the Holocaust museum

Chapter 3: The First Intifada

On December 9, 1987, an Israel Defense Forces (IDF) truck collided with a Palestinian car in Gaza's Jabalya refugee camp, killing four civilians. It sparked the first Palestinian *Intifada* (shaking off), an uprising that captured the world's attention and lasted into 1991 and the Madrid peace talks, which in turn led to the 1993 Oslo Accords. As with so many other events in the Palestinian-Israeli situation, the kindling had already been prepared by growing anger and resentment about the ongoing occupation and needed only that spark to burst into flame.

Comfortably ensconced in Philadelphia with my teaching at Friends' Central School and with the research for my Ph.D. dissertation completed, I initially paid little attention to the first news reports out of Palestine and Israel. I hadn't been back since '79 and had not maintained close contact with friends and former students in Ramallah. But the *Intifada* gathered steam, and the growing attention in the media to the grassroots Palestinian movement to "shake off" the occupation, Israel's violent response in trying to stop the uprising, and concern for how old friends were doing in Ramallah drew me in.

The more I followed the unfolding drama, the more I wanted to return to Ramallah to see how the uprising was affecting my friends. I talked it over with Jane and decided to see if it might be possible to go back to Palestine in the summer of '88.

I contacted my old friend and housemate, Donn Hutchison, to see if I could stay with him at Swift House, his residence since marrying Sina, and still his home with his children after her death. I also got in touch with Nabil Ajlouny, a member of the Ramallah Friends Meeting and the district manager for KLM Airlines, to see what tickets would cost.

Preliminaries accomplished, I applied for a Clayton L. Farraday Master Teachership Program grant at Friends' Central. The grant was named after a much-loved former teacher at FCS and enabled faculty members to have mini-sabbaticals for pursuing special interests. The school granted me the fellowship, and amid tears from Jane and our three children, and some fear and trepidation on my part, I departed for Tel Aviv on July 24, 1988.

The entry in my journal from that first day indicated that I was not feeling anxious about the coming two weeks' sojourn, but that "today's *Herald Tribune* noted that two more Palestinians had been killed." I do recall that as I looked out of the plane's window as Israel's coastline appeared, I thought to myself, "What on earth am I getting myself into?" Descriptions of the Intifada in the American press had depicted violence and carnage.

As I arrived in Ramallah after the hour's journey from the airport, I was surprised by how different it looked. Many stores were shuttered; a major restaurant I remembered had gone out of business; the streets were quiet; painted over graffiti was everywhere; the cinemas were gone; even the *manara*, Ramallah's central round-about, had been replaced by straight drive-throughs. But Swift House was the same, and after catching up with Donn and many old friends who stopped by that evening, I went to sleep in my old room.

During my first full day, I wandered the town, noting again how many shops were closed, including the ice cream shop owned by the family of my former student, Ihsan Rukab. The meetinghouse had been abandoned, its roof collapsing from years of wear and tear from weather and war. Its once lovely yard was overgrown and trash-strewn. At the girls school, I saw many former colleagues and one former student, Jirius Abu El-Etham, now a math teacher there. Our conversation was about the mundane tasks of running a school in abnormal circumstances, but beneath the surface was the Intifada. Everyone expressed real pride in the gains made in continuing the uprising for this long and not buckling to the intense pressure from Israel. I also noted in my journal, "All with whom I have talked have only one objective: self-determination. There is no sense of bitterness or hatred; gone is the old breast-beating and depression."

I also stopped by the boys school and again saw old friends and former students, noting that one of the areas of the campus I remembered as being unused had been turned into a vegetable garden, one of many Intifada gardens I saw throughout Ramallah and El-Bireh as part of the attempt to shake free of dependence on Israeli commodities. People had also taken to using old cisterns and kerosene lanterns to gain independence from the Israeli water and electric systems. Strikes, demonstrations, tax refusal, and other actions were part of the nonviolent resistance—as was even the simple gesture of displaying the Palestinian flag, banned by Israel. On one occasion, Palestinians made thousands of flags, attached them to string with rocks on both ends and tossed them over light wires overnight. The next morning, soldiers had to spend hours taking them down, often by firing their machine guns at the fluttering symbols of Palestinian identity.

An Intifada garden near the Friends Girls School.

Back at Swift House, I talked for a long time with Donn as he shared about the difficulties of the recent years—the loss of Sina, his own father, Sina's father, and other disappointments. He talked about how he was drawing closer to embracing Islam and its sense of God's absolute sovereignty—that all is a part of God's plan and can't be changed. Moreover, he said, Muslims had been the most supportive during his times of need.

That evening, we had supper at Swift House with John and Jennifer Bing-Canar, American teachers at the schools. Jennifer shared the story of being hit by a rubber bullet fired by an IDF soldier. Witnessing a demonstration in Ramallah with John, they had followed soldiers who were beating two teenage girls. When the soldiers headed for a building, she feared for them and continued to follow until some women began throwing stones at them. She decided to leave before it became a dangerous incident, but as she was departing, one of the soldiers shot her in the back and came running up to her and John as she lay flat on the ground and yelled, "Nazi, Nazi—you have no right to be here!"

All Palestinian schools had been closed by Israel, and in the meantime, Jennifer and John began working for the Save the Children organization. They had documented more than three-thousand cases of children hospitalized for injuries incurred in clashes, with twenty-four killed by tear gas alone. Many others had been killed by stray bullets while playing.

At day's end, I commented in my journal, "People go about the day's business as any would anywhere, but with a new sense of solidarity, hope, and purpose. The surface calm masks an underlying determination to stick it out."

As I continued to wander about the city on visits and errands, I noticed the increased Israeli military presence. During my previous times in Ramallah, the IDF was visible mostly on jeep patrols through the city and the night incursions such as one near Swift House in '72 when the army expelled a family for alleged participation in the resistance, sealed the windows, and filled the house with poured concrete. Now I saw constant army foot patrols and snipers on the tops of many of the taller buildings.

Conversations continued to reveal strong emotions. As I chatted in my broken Arabic with the family that helped maintain the grounds of the boys school, the Muslim mother brought me Arabic coffee, chocolates, and sweets as she shared her belief that God is the same for all people and that she was sorry for the loss of life in the Intifada. To her, it was immaterial whether they were Jewish or Palestinian. "*Kul hum haram,*" she said. "It is a shame for any to die."

I also saw that several new restaurants had been opened in Ramallah; during my earlier times in the city, there were only two: Na'oum's and the Grand Hotel. But all were closed as people felt it wasn't politic to celebrate or eat out during this time. Still, as soldiers looked on from the rooftops and walked through the streets on regular patrols, life went on. Donn's son had friends over to play computer games. His daughter went out to buy bread, running home crying as she was chased by a stray dog. Although Israel had closed the schools, trying to stem the tide of young people organizing, children continued to study. Teachers and administrators had organized a way to get them packets of lessons to do each week. Although Israel's closure of the schools lasted more than a year, students maintained their studies.

Donn also shared how he tried to keep his children out of harm's way amid the enormous pressure to join in the resistance to the occupation. One time he learned that his son had participated in throwing rocks at an IDF jeep. After his confrontation with such military might, the boy was spanked at home for defying orders not to participate in rock-throwing.

Many years later, after his son had moved to the States, married, and was working in Pennsylvania, he was having a drink at a bar after work when another patron approached him and asked him where he was from. Leery of saying he was from Palestine at a time of heightened tensions following the attacks of September 11, 2001, he kept hedging until the man pulled out of him that he was from Ramallah. "I thought so," said the man, as he pulled the hair back from a scar on his forehead. "I was in the Israeli army during the first Intifada, and one day you threw a rock that hit me here!" Donn's son examined the scar and responded, "Looks like my work!" The two had a laugh and continued to drink together.

All were worried about their children. Soldiers used to aim for the feet of demonstrators, but now they aimed for the chest. Israel's Defense Minister Yitzhak Rabin had ordered the army to "break the bones" of protesters. In the boys school, there was a bulletin board with paper cutouts of student hands accompanying the statement, "Stop breaking our hands." Two teachers told me of being hit by rubber bullets; children had jaws and eyes blown out by those bullets. I had picked several up off the street—metal balls with a thin coat of rubber and hard cylinders of rubber, all fired at high velocity. It was easy to see how they could cause such grievous injury and even death.

A bulletin board in the Friends Boys School protesting the Israeli policy of breaking the bones of protesters.

Back from work in outlying villages with Save the Children, Jennifer and John told further stories of the impact of the Intifada. They had seen olive groves bulldozed by the IDF and heard of children beaten on their way to school; others had been killed by snipers. "Ramallah hasn't seen the real Intifada," they said. "Reporters haven't gotten into the villages."

We all wondered how such direct knowledge of atrocities could be shared back in the States, given how profound the denial and disbelief were there. It was agreed that the best approach would be simply to make human rights the issue and not get into the dead-end debate of who had killed the most people. The American workers expressed their own struggle to keep from hating the oppressor while marveling at how little bitterness and hatred they witnessed in the Palestinians.

As my second full day in Ramallah ended, I wrote in my journal that "the more children who are killed, the more orchards bulldozed, the more people beaten, the more difficult it will be for the Palestinians to forget and forgive, and their resolve will stiffen."

On my third day, I traveled to Jerusalem by service, the local public taxi. Travel was still easy, as checkpoints had yet to be constructed. I visited the *Kotel*, the Western Wall, the holiest site in Judaism, and marveled at how many Jewish tourists were still coming, many for bar mitzvahs. Worshipers thronged in with tambourines, bells, and drums—dancing exuberantly with arms extended like charismatics as they observed the Psalmist's directive to "enter my gates with thanksgiving and my courts with praise."

I wandered the old, familiar ways through the Old City, enjoying the sights, sounds, and smells of the *souk* (market). Along the way, an Israeli soldier, no more than eighteen or nineteen, invited me to take his picture as he posed with a rifle in his lap, laughing, and eating *khubbiz*, the Arabic bread. I saw other soldiers speaking Arabic kindly with little children while others patrolled more tentatively with live magazines in their weapons.

As I left through Damascus Gate to go to the KLM office to meet Nabeel Ajlouny, I noticed that the Arab shops were all shuttering at noon. When I arrived at Nabeel's office, he, too, was pulling the metal shutter down over the entrance. He explained to me that the weekly *bayan*, a newsletter from the underground leadership of the Intifada orchestrating resistance actions, had called for shops that day to open at 9:00 a.m. and close precisely at noon. It was a display of defiance, even while the IDF often welded shut the shops of those who complied. All through the West Bank and Gaza, shops were closing in unison.

Nabeel Ajlouny closing his office on a strike day.

As Nabeel drove me back to Ramallah in his car, he spoke of how amazed he was by the discipline the Palestinians were showing. "This is new with us," he said. "There is a tremendous sense of solidarity, and now the abnormal situation of coordinated closings and strike days is becoming normal. There is no way we will return to the status quo."

Nabeel's description of the Intifada and the Palestinians' ability to maintain it for so many months—and overwhelmingly nonviolently even in the face of incredible military force and brutality—gave me the impression that the Palestinians were developing a sense of confidence and even a feeling of moral superiority in the way they were conducting their resistance.

For the first time during my visit, I heard from Nabeel a hope for an independent Palestinian state rather than a return to Jordan if the occupation ended. "We have taken control of our own destiny now," he said, "and I am confident that Israelis and Palestinians can get along if there is a state. Israel's argument that they need to control the West Bank and Gaza for security is no longer valid in an era of long-distance missiles."

Nabeel also mentioned that the secretary in his office was a first cousin to the seventeen-year old Palestinian boy shot to death while riding his bicycle in Jerusalem the previous week. An IDF reservist was being held for questioning about the incident.

Back in Ramallah, I met with Khalil Mahshi, the principal of the boys school who had assumed the position when Fuad Zaru retired. He echoed much of what Nabeel had said. "It has reached the point of no return. The status quo is no longer possible." But he expressed the fear that if Israel continued its violent response to the uprising, Palestinians would find it harder and harder to maintain their nonviolent actions. He mentioned an incident in a neighboring village the day before when soldiers broke into a house, beat two boys, knocked their mother unconscious, and were preparing to shoot tear gas and rubber bullets when Palestinians intervened to stop the attack.

Beyond his concerns about Israel's violent response to the Intifada, Khalil shared his worry that the Palestinian leadership in exile, the PLO, might return in a future peace accord and take the reins of government. Raised mostly in the Palestinian diaspora and not part of the grassroots Intifada, not to mention being trained fighters, the PLO would be out-of-step with the local culture and philosophy of resistance. His fear was that they would impose the kind of government that would be antithetical to the secular, democratic, and non-militarized Palestine he desired.

As I contemplated the differences between 1988 and my experience in Ramallah from 1970 to 1972 and even the visit in '79, I remembered that in the early '70s the people were angry and depressed but made no effort to resist the occupation. In '79, the depression was deeper, owing to the ascendancy of the Likud Party, Menachem Begin, and the construction of Israeli settlements in Gaza and the West Bank, but there was still little active resistance. In 1988, however, although nothing had yet been gained, thousands had been injured, and already more than two hundred killed. With major inconvenience and Israel's continued intransigence, the Palestinians were acting together with discipline and purpose, almost euphorically.

Would Israel grasp the opportunity for a resolution to the conflict or try to maintain total control? Many feared that if they didn't seize the moment but chose to crush the Intifada outwardly, the resistance would turn inward and become violent.

July 29 was a strike day as directed by the weekly *bayan*. There was nearly total compliance with the call for shop closings (except for pharmacies and medical facilities) and a halt in all transportation. It was eerily quiet and calm.

I visited with Jean Zaru, new clerk of the Friends meeting and widow of the former principal of the boys school. She talked about a recent visit to a refugee camp and how empty it was of young men—nearly all were in prison. The women were gathering wood to bake bread when soldiers took it away, fearing demonstrations. The women then tried to bake with rags, but soldiers came and put out the fires. Finally, secretively, they succeeded in making bread. One of them told Jean proudly, "The Israelis are so frustrated. They can't subdue us!"

Jean went on to comment about how the Intifada was spawning an Arab renaissance. People were becoming inventive, cooperative, and clever. Boys, girls, and women were feeling empowered, and things would never go back to how they once were. As women experienced power, and students challenged the authority of soldiers, they would not be satisfied with former power dynamics socially or in the classroom.

At supper that evening back at Swift House, Donn's children told a story of how the first time their father left them alone after Sina's death, two soldiers entered the house looking for something and asked where their father was. They told them he had gone shopping, and then the soldiers asked where their mother was. Not wanting to reveal that they were alone, they said she was in the shower. But when the soldiers noticed that the bathroom door was open, they asked why they had lied.

"You aren't afraid of us, are you?" one of the soldiers asked. "You needn't be. We don't shoot little people!"

In unison, Donn's children blurted out to us, "Why did *they* lie?!"

Donn's daughter, Rana, models a resistance T-shirt. The farmer is cutting down stalks of wheat with a sickle, each stalk representing an individual person—under each stalk is the Arabic *ana* (I). On the farmer's back is the Arabic *Nahnu* (we). The message is that we are stronger together. The cartoonist Naji Ali's "Handala" character watches, characteristically with his back turned.

On my first Sunday in Ramallah, I attended the Friends meeting for worship, now held in a room at the girls school since the condition of the meetinghouse made it unsuitable for use. The continuing impact of the political and economic situation on the Christian population was acutely felt. With a history of more education and closer ties to the West than the Muslim population, Christians emigrated at much higher numbers as conditions deteriorated. In the early '70s, the Friends meeting enjoyed a regular attendance in the mid-30s. That morning, there were five—two American teachers, a visiting Jewish Quaker, one Palestinian Quaker, and myself.

Jean Zaru had invited me to lunch, and after worship I headed that way on foot. Soon I noticed that shops were suddenly shuttering, even though it was a day when they were to remain open. Looking down a side street, I soon realized why.

The street had been barricaded by stones and burning tires, and everyone knew that meant Israeli soldiers would soon arrive.

In rapid succession, foot soldiers appeared, followed by jeeps; then several Palestinian boys darted out from behind a wall and pelted the soldiers with rocks, disappearing just as suddenly. Shots rang out, and soldiers started fanning out to question anyone in the streets. Two members of the boys school staff saw me watching the action and cautioned me that I had better move on if I didn't want to be commandeered by the soldiers to clear the barricades.

I moved on.

The scene on the way to Jean Zaru's home

Lunch at Jean's with Leroy, a staff member of the Mennonite Central Committee working in the West Bank, was wonderful, and as we began dessert, we had a surprise guest: Landrum Bolling! Following his retirement at Earlham College and subsequent work with the Lilly Foundation, he had assumed the position of director at Tantur, a Roman Catholic ecumenical institute between Jerusalem and Bethlehem.

Landrum spoke with us about his hope for Christian, Jewish, and Muslim dialogue that went deeper than the usual courtesy roundtables. He critiqued Christian involvement in the Middle East, saying it needed to move beyond humanitarian aid to "bearing witness" in the situation.

Talking with Leroy, Landrum praised the MCC's work in West Bank agriculture to develop farming associations and expand markets. But he also noted that the work had met with Israeli resistance, since highly subsidized Israeli goods were dumped in the West Bank while Arab goods could not be exported. The MCC had contracts signed between European wholesalers and Palestinian farmers, but Israel stood in the way. I had heard a similar story from a former student of mine, Suheir, now married to the principal of the boys school. To encourage women's empowerment and self-sufficiency, she had partnered with others in starting Karameesh, a sweater knitting business. They recruited women to work on creating the items, and they had even obtained foreign markets for them, but Israel would not allow export of the sweaters.

Suheir modeling one of the women's co-op sweaters.

Leroy mentioned that a man recently killed by IDF soldiers in an execution-style shooting was the son of the cook at the Mennonite school in Beit Jala, near Bethlehem.

As I walked back to Swift House, I noticed that the scene of the earlier clash had been completely cleared. Passing by the Israeli police station next to the boys school, I saw that soldiers were interrogating about a dozen young men who stood in the sun with their arms over their heads.

The next day, the first of two consecutive announced strike days, I walked through deserted streets to the meetinghouse to work on cleaning up the yard. Although the building was no longer being used for worship, I wanted to make the depressing scene a bit more presentable.

The yard was a sad sight; rubble filled one side of it where a road had been widened. Abandoned stoves, broken concrete, bent railings, bottles, and mounds of trash littered the once pristine area. I set about placing the stones against the walls surrounding the yard and filled trash bags with debris. After several hours of work, I thought it looked a little better.

While I was working, a jeep pulled up, and one of the soldiers asked me who I was and where I worked. I gave my name and responded that I worked in Philadelphia. "But we're not in Philadelphia, Max Carter!" he answered. I then explained why I was there, and he asked for identification. As I showed him my passport, I asked if I could take his picture "as a souvenir." He good-naturedly replied, "No. I would have to break your camera."

For several days, I continued to do various chores around Swift House—whitewashing the kitchen, working in the garden, trimming overgrown vegetation—and listened to the news of ongoing conflict on Jordanian, English, and Israeli radio and TV, noting the differences in reporting of the same events.

The news was seldom good, no matter who was reporting. One day the IDF blew up ten Palestinian homes and sealed two others because family members were suspected of resistance activity. Several Palestinians were killed each day in clashes, rocks and Molotov cocktails proving no match for Israel's arsenal of weapons. Feisal Husseini, the father of a boys school student and a prominent political figure in Palestinian society, had been arrested, and many feared he would be deported as Israel continued its futile attempt to ferret out the leadership of the Intifada.

The one piece of good news, that King Hussein had ceded Jordanian claims to the West Bank, was itself tinged with skepticism. Many suspected it was a ploy by the king to see the Palestinians fail to organize into a viable independent entity and beg him to return in an agreement with Israel. There was no love lost for the king. In my first year in Ramallah, the Jordanian dinar was still in circulation, and when I paid for some groceries with the currency, the shop keeper pointed to the likeness of Hussein on the bill and asked if I knew who he was. "King Hussein," I answered. "No!" the man responded adamantly. "King DOG!"

On August 3, I went into Jerusalem again. I walked into Jewish West Jerusalem to tour Yad Vashem, the Holocaust museum.

Moving from Arab East Jerusalem into Jewish West Jerusalem, though divided only by a street, was like traveling from one world into another. West Jerusalem was, indeed, the West; one could very well be in any American city, apart from the predominant Arab architecture left over from before 1948. But what struck me this time more than anything else was that there were no patrolling soldiers, no jeeps, no snipers strategically placed on the tops of buildings. It was a different world, one I didn't feel fully comfortable in.

I underestimated the distance to Yad Vashem, and by the time I covered the several miles to the museum in August heat, I was dehydrated and faint. But even before finding a drinking fountain, I began exploring the various parts of the complex: the memorial to the 1.5 million children killed, the display of the various concentration camps, the exhibit of scenes from the Warsaw ghetto. It was a moving experience, but, along with the stark reminder of humanity's capacity for inhuman behavior, I was struck by impressions that Yad Vashem certainly did not intend to convey.

The pictures of the children lost in the Holocaust looked very much like the children in Ramallah. Many of the photos from the Warsaw ghetto with trucks full of helmeted soldiers patrolling the area while residents went about their daily business could have been Ramallah, minus Warsaw's street cars.

A video depicting how the Germans had closed the Jewish schools under the pretext of typhus struck me as ironic, given that Israel had just closed the Palestinian schools on the pretext that they were staging grounds for the resistance. The photos of tattooed Jews reminded me of Jewish Defense League founder Meir Kahane's call for tattooing Palestinians so they could be told apart from Israelis. At least that proposal was met with overwhelming opposition from Holocaust survivors who remembered what tattoos meant for them.

After touring the museum, I grabbed something to eat and drink and walked the two hours back to East Jerusalem, avoiding the ample public transportation. From there I took a service back to Ramallah, arriving in time to get cleaned up and attend mid-week meeting with the Quaker community.

The following day, I heard on the news that a 57-year old Arab-American man had died of a heart attack in the neighboring village of Beitin after soldiers had forced him to clean up graffiti someone had painted on his wall. I decided to walk to the village to see how people were reacting.

In the village, I chatted with a group of friendly boys who were eager to have me take their picture as they flashed the peace sign. I also talked with some of the adults, gathering the impression that none were displaying bitterness or anger. I did ask them, though, what they thought of an idea circulating in Ramallah that Palestinians should recognize Israel on its seventy-eight percent of the historical British Palestine Mandate and accept a Palestinian state on the remaining twenty-two percent, the West Bank and Gaza.

"Oh, no; it would never work," they said. "If you give Israel an inch, they will take a mile and toss us into the desert!"

Returning to Ramallah, I passed by an Israeli army base. Seeing a soldier standing guard at the entrance, I approached him and asked what he thought of the idea circulating among the Palestinians that they recognize Israel and accept a Palestinian state in the West Bank and Gaza.

"Oh, no," he responded. "You can't trust the Palestinians. They would drive us into the sea." I asked him what could be hoped for then. "The Arabs have to go," he said.

Back at Swift House, I shared the experience with a Palestinian woman visiting while she took a break from doctoral studies in the States. When I told her of the soldier's comments, she said that in her more than twenty years of living in Palestine, even coming from a small, rural village, she had never heard a Palestinian talk about driving Jews into the sea. She had heard it in other Arab countries, but never among Palestinians. "Meanwhile, Israel has driven us into the desert."

News continued to carry the daily accounts of arrests, home demolitions, deaths, speculation about King Hussein's intentions, and whether Faisal Husseini could be implicated in anything that would warrant his deportation. The *Jerusalem Post* carried an article by Rehavam Ze'evi, a former military officer nicknamed Gandhi who advocated "transfer" of all Palestinians out of the occupied territories. In 2001 during the second Intifada, he was Minister of Tourism in Israel and was assassinated by a member of the Popular Front for the Liberation of Palestine.

Palestinians debated what Jordan's cutting ties with the West Bank would mean. Some saw it as an opportunity right-wingers in Israel would use to extend Israeli law into the West Bank and eventually annex the territory. Others cited Prime Minister Shamir's stated opposition to annexation. Some hoped that it would lead to a recognition of the PLO as the sole bargaining partner for the Palestinians in future peace negotiations.

My work cleaning the yard at the meetinghouse continued, along with other odd jobs like moving a piano a European teacher at the Friends School had purchased for $1,200 from a Russian Jewish immigrant in an Israeli settlement. I learned that it was a common practice for Russian Jews to bring pianos with them to sell, since they were not allowed to take much money out with them.

Toward the end of my time in Ramallah, I had supper with the principal of the boys school and his wife and had the opportunity to talk at length with them again. Khalil talked about the difficulties of trying to fund a school with tuition payments when most parents were hard-pressed at the time to bring home enough pay simply to maintain their home. In addition, soldiers frequently came to the school threatening to close it permanently because of suspected resistance activity by students. After several demanding visits by the army, Khalil finally told the soldiers, "Go ahead. You can do anything you want to. You have the guns. You have the power. Just know that this isn't good for the relations between our two peoples."

For her part, Suheir said that most of her former classmates at Bir Zeit University were in jail, and everyone knew someone in prison, hurt, or killed. She feared that if the Intifada continued, the Israelis would become even more violent. At the same time, though, she felt that Israeli attitudes about Palestinians were changing. Before the Intifada, they despised Arabs and looked down on them as inferior and useful only as menial labor. With the Intifada, they were having to confront a different Arab—confident, resilient, creative, and proud.

Such discussions and my time in Ramallah had left me with a mixture of optimism and sadness. People spoke so hopefully about a future state of their own. They were so proud of the Intifada, even with its hardships. Coming out of their self-imposed mourning period after '67, Palestinians were dancing, expressing themselves artistically, re-claiming their heritage. Yet there was no indication from Israel that would give credence to those hopes and celebrations. People the age of my former students were ready for a two-state solution, the same students who eighteen years ago wouldn't even say the word "Israel." But would Israel give up the dream that many of its citizens had of holding on to the West Bank and Gaza?

Feisal Husseini's earlier arrest had occurred the day after he had given a speech to Peace Now in West Jerusalem—a speech in which he had advocated for a two-state solution and coexistence.

On my last morning in Ramallah, I said my final goodbyes to Donn and his family and traveled to Jerusalem to stay at the home of Nancy Nye, the principal of the Friends Girls

School, so I could be assured of getting to the airport the next day in case of a closure or strike in the Palestinian territories.

Nancy claimed that I was responsible for her coming to Ramallah and working at the girls school. While a counselor at Richmond High School in Indiana, she heard me speak at Earlham about my experience in Ramallah, and she determined that if the opportunity ever arose, she would apply to work at the Friends schools.

When she did become principal of the girls school, she met and married Mubarak Awad, a Palestinian Christian born in East Jerusalem. As a youth, he was influenced by his pacifist mother, as well as by Mennonite and Quaker missionaries, to adopt nonviolence. Attending college at the Mennonite Bluffton College in Ohio, he learned about Mahatma Gandhi and began developing a philosophy of nonviolence that could be applied to Palestinian resistance to the occupation. In 1983, he returned to Jerusalem and established the Palestinian Center for the Study of Nonviolence.

Mubarak's advocacy of nonviolent strategies gained little traction among Palestinians. He was American-educated, he was a Christian, and his particular strategies had not been tried before, even though there was a long tradition in Palestine of unarmed popular resistance to various occupations.

Nancy shared with me how the Israelis had blundered by making Mubarak a national hero and calling attention to his strategies when he was deported in June of 1988 as Israel was growing concerned about the means of resistance being employed in the Intifada. Before the Intifada, Mubarak couldn't give away his posters and translations of nonviolence scholar Gene Sharp's writings. After Israel's attempts to silence him, there was so much demand for them that they quickly went out of print.

Nancy also shared some of the research that the Center for the Study of Nonviolence had done in the first eight months of the Intifada. The Center found that 95.1 percent of Palestinian actions were specifically nonviolent. The weekly *bayans* uniformly called for nonviolent action: strikes, demonstrations, praying and fasting, developing alternative institutions, withholding taxes, raising the Palestinian flag, boycotting Israeli products, boycotting Israeli employment, resignations from positions, defying school closings, writing articles condemning the occupation, refusal to pay fines, breaking curfews, blocking roads, and even ringing bells.

The nonviolent nature of the beginning of the Intifada, however, is disputed by many. Focus is given to the stone-throwing and Molotov cocktails, even though that was a tiny fraction of the actions. For their part, many Palestinians came to avoid using the term "nonviolent," as the response by Israel was anything but nonviolent. "Popular resistance" would become the more apt description.

Nancy also shared the story of U.S. Congressman Steven Solarz's visit to Mubarak's office during a trip to Jerusalem. A Jew from New York, Solarz was interested in talking about Rabin's policy of "breaking bones." Mubarak told him that it was still going on, but the Congressman replied that he had been told by Israeli military commanders that any beatings were random and the fault of individuals. Mubarak was able to show him evidence to the contrary. "You mean the Military Command lied to me?" Solarz said. "Yes," was Mubarak's answer. Later in Congress, Rep. Solarz gave testimony that Israel's Military Command had misrepresented facts.

While in Jerusalem, I walked again into West Jerusalem to visit a favorite bookstore, Steimatzky's. While there, I browsed through a book on international terrorism edited by Benjamin Netanyahu. In it, he defined terrorism in terms of directing action against innocent civilians for the purpose of achieving political ends. I thought of the nearly two hundred Palestinians who had already died in the Intifada—overwhelmingly unarmed civilians.

Later, I caught a few hours of sleep and was up by 2:00 a.m. to catch an Israeli taxi to the airport. While en route, I asked the driver what he thought of the notion of a two-state solution. "I am an eleventh generation Israeli," he replied. "Jews and Arabs lived together before, and they must live together. A Palestinian state doesn't concern me."

When I returned home safe and sound, I learned that my family had been very worried. The children continually asked Jane if she would re-marry if I were killed, and the fact that they didn't hear from me the entire time I was away didn't help. All the letters and postcards I had sent from Ramallah arrived after I had already returned home.

At Friends' Central, I wrote about my experience for the Fall 1988 issue of the Friends' Central *Forum*, a new publication that sought to communicate the activities and interests of members of the FCS community. After describing a summary of my trip, I wrote, "I did personally throw rocks, paint walls, and shed blood during the Intifada. But it was while clearing the yard at the meetinghouse, sprucing up school property, and ripping out cactus from an overgrown garden."

More seriously, I ended my essay with the statement, "Most people in the West Bank spend days in mundane activity, overshadowed by a military occupation now entering its twenty-second year. All share the dream that one day soon, a normal day in Ramallah will be spent pursuing the activities of shopping, worshiping, working, and caring for children free of the abnormal oversight of military power."

I was not visited by a representative of the Jewish Federation when the essay appeared. I did, however, have interesting conversations with the *Forum* editor, the FCS librarian and school parent who also happened to be Jewish.

And I gained some credibility with my FCS colleagues when I reported that, as I had heard in Ramallah, the PLO would recognize Israel that November and call for a two-state solution. Right on cue that November, it happened.

Chapter 4: Between the Intifadas

After completing my Ph.D. at Temple University and surviving at Friends' Central School after writing about my summer in Ramallah during the first Intifada, I accepted a position at Guilford College in Greensboro, North Carolina. Our family moved in 1990, and I took up the work of establishing the college's first official office of campus ministry.

Early in my time at Guilford, I began to develop a Quaker leadership program that would involve a trip to Palestine and Israel. Such a trip would expose students to Friends in the Middle East and challenge their comfortable American Quaker ideas by showing the conditions in which Palestinian Quakers live. I also wanted to see how they analyzed the political situation in terms of their commitment to Friends testimonies of peace and equality.

The college supported my plans to organize a summer service-learning trip for that purpose, and funds from the Friends Center I directed on campus could underwrite student expenses. The Friends Schools in Ramallah agreed to host us. The first trip planned in 1994, however, was scuttled when violence broke out following Baruch Goldstein's murder of twenty-nine worshipers in Hebron's Ibrahimi Mosque. Yitzhak Rabin's assassination and riots following Israel's announcement of plans to build a tunnel under the Muslim Quarter next to the *Kotel* in East Jerusalem ended plans for trips in '95 and '96. But we finally went in the summer of

'97 with a group that included six Guilford students, a Duke University student, and our three children.

Seeing Ramallah for the first time since the summer of '88 was a shock to me. Before the Oslo Accords in '93 led to the establishment of the Palestinian National Authority and giddy hopes for peace, Ramallah was a rather sleepy city. We used to joke that the stone sidewalks were rolled up by 9:00 p.m. each night. But with Yasser Arafat's taking up residence at the old British fortress complex in Ramallah/El-Bireh—where my continued presence had been equated with Phantom jets—Ramallah had become the *de facto* capital of the emerging Palestinian state. Consulates and embassies dotted the outskirts of the city, and the Manara had been reconstructed in glorious fashion. The streets were crowded, high-end shops dotted Main (Rukab) Street, and multi-storied buildings had been built on top of the former, low-lying shops. Foreign investment had poured in, transforming the city.

We settled in at the Friends Boys School for our three-week work camp. We cleared brush, moved dirt, and transformed an area around a newly constructed science building into an area that later would be festooned with green grass and fruit trees. We shoveled loads of gravel and moved boulders for the construction of a new driveway. We chiseled off plaster from walls, exposing the lovely native limestone of the classrooms.

Although the meetinghouse had been abandoned by 1997, we worked on cleaning the yard of trash and weeds.

Jane (left), Seth (center), and Lissa (right) tackle a pile of dirt at the Boys School campus.

Joining us were some students from the Friends School and two from the Evangelical School. They talked with us about how the military occupation had truncated their childhood and how they had to face the harsh realities of the political situation. And several shared the feeling after the first day of labor that Quakers worked far too hard. Only two returned the second day—the two from the Evangelical School.

The work camp, organized in Ramallah by two young American teachers, provided ample opportunity for work and a little exposure to the Palestinian leadership arising there. We met with noted human rights attorney Jonathan Kuttab who gave us his thoughts on what might develop in the emerging situation post-Oslo. He envisioned three possible outcomes: one side would eradicate the other, two separate states would develop, or one state would be created with shared land and equal rights.

Jonathan was not optimistic about Israel's willingness to compromise or in the West's willingness to hold Israel to high moral standards of conduct in human rights. He felt that conditions change only when people take a stand based on morals and ethics rather than on calculating their chances of winning. He urged Quakers to take the moral high ground in addressing the situation and focus on proclaiming what is right, rather than worrying about being effective.

On a visit to the new and very modern campus of Birzeit University near Ramallah, we were told by one of the staff members that reconciliation with Israel would be difficult, given the lack of rights enjoyed by Palestinians, even with the Oslo Accords. This theme continued to be expressed by other Palestinians, a rather sobering reminder that all the new construction and modern amenities masked a situation that many did not find hopeful. Later at the Sabeel Center in Jerusalem, a Christian center for the promotion of Palestinian liberation theology, we were told about the ongoing struggle of the Palestinian people for basic human rights. We also learned about extremist settlers and the "holes in the Swiss cheese" partitioning of Palestinian areas in the West Bank as a result of the Oslo agreements—a reality that would make an autonomous Palestinian state very difficult.

Israelis we met with offered a somewhat brighter picture. Yehezkel Landau, a former student of Guilford President William R. Rogers, met us at the Mennonite Central Committee's office in Jerusalem and told us about his wife Dalia's history. Bulgarian Jewish immigrants to Israel after '48, her family had been given a home in Ramla formerly owned by Palestinians who had to flee when Israeli forces captured the city. They were not told of the previous owners and settled in. After the '67 war, however, they one day received visitors from Ramallah—the former residents of the house. They especially wanted to see a lemon tree they had planted in the courtyard.

Yehezkel related how Dalia went on to be involved in turning the home that had once been Palestinian, and then Israeli, into "Open House," a center for reconciliation and addressing the needs of the impoverished remaining Palestinian Arabs in Ramla. The story of that encounter and subsequent use of the residence became the popular book *The Lemon Tree* by Sandy Tolan. Yehezkel went on to share, however, that his own optimism was being shaken by Prime Minister Netanyahu's avowed desire to destroy the Oslo Accords.

Ron Kronish of Israel's Interreligious Coordinating Council spoke with us about cooperative ventures in Israel among Jews, Christians, and Muslims. And at Neve Shalom/ Wahat al-Salam, an intentional community of Israeli Arabs and Jews living together on former lands of the Latrun monastery, we experienced the possibility of co-existence but heard of how difficult it was—even among those dedicated to the task—to overcome the differences in Israel of how Jews and non-Jews relate to each other. Even the ubiquitous concept of military service, required of Jews but not of Arabs, served to underline the difficulty. In times of conflict, when some community members were off fighting, others remained behind, resentful that their former friends were possibly killing relatives elsewhere.

Time with a rabbi talking about the Talmud, worship with Friends in Ramallah, outings to the Galilee and the Dead Sea Valley, conversations with people in Ramallah, wandering the streets of Jerusalem and Ramallah, and more work added to our experience. It wasn't clear whether the Oslo peace process would work, but it was very apparent that things would never be the same again, just as Ramallah would never be the sleepy place I remembered.

It was on a visit to Hebron, though, that the reality of the situation really hit home. Visiting with members of the Christian Peacemaker Teams (CPT), a Christian group invited by Palestinians in the city who wanted accompaniment in their conflict with a group of Israeli settlers, we experienced some of the worst of the occupation. Followers of rabbis Abraham Isaac Kook and Meir Kahane, these settlers in the heart of the city were terrorizing residents. Iron mesh covered the market streets to try to keep the settlers who had taken over the top floors of several buildings from tossing rocks and garbage on the shoppers below. USAid was pouring millions of dollars into improving the streets and infrastructure of the main market area of Hebron to encourage the peace process, but the settlers were trying to make it uninhabitable for the Palestinians.

After learning about the situation from the CPT members in their apartment, we accompanied them to a meeting with the Muslim Youth League. The stores were closed, and the streets were empty—until a violent confrontation flared up between IDF troops and Palestinian *shabaab* (young people) in an adjacent street, a mere half block away. Soldiers in riot gear were firing tear gas, rubber bullets, and live ammunition at the youth at the other end of the street; they, in turn, were hurling rocks and Molotov cocktails.

It was a surreal scene. As the conflict raged, members of the international press stood along the sides of the street, boom mics picking up the sounds of the clash while some were interviewing participants in small clumps up and down the street. As we stood in amazement, an IDF patrol approached us. In a distinctive Midwestern American accent, the patrol leader said, "This is a closed military zone! What are you doing here?"

I pointed to our two CPT guides, wearing their distinctive red caps, and said, "We're with the people in the red hats." The leader then turned to them and asked the same question. Kathy, one of the Quaker CPT members, explained, "We're with the Christian Peacemaker Teams, and we are here to get in 'the way of Jesus'—and get in the way of violence."

The patrol leader sent us on our way saying, "Well, this is not the time nor the place for peacemaking!"

The last morning in Ramallah, another experience brought home the vanishing past of the place. We wandered out into the *wadi* east of the city to watch the sunrise, just as we had watched the sunset earlier in the valley west of the city. As the dawn broke over the still-pristine countryside, it felt almost as if we were in a biblical landscape. Quail flew by; foxes and gazelles scampered about over the rocks. But above the valley on the hill named *Jabal Taweel* (long mountain), grazing land when I lived in Ramallah in the '70s, was a new Israeli settlement.

Ramallah's explosive growth would fill the western *wadi* in years to come, and the sewage and garbage from the settlement would fill the eastern valley. As the open areas continued to vanish, they would come to symbolize for me the vanishing hopes and cautious optimism of the years after Oslo.

It wasn't as long between visits for me to Ramallah/El-Bireh the next time. Maia, our oldest daughter, was hooked on Palestine after three weeks—defying her Great-Great Aunt Annice's theory that it took two years there to develop a habit of returning. Following college graduation in '98, she accepted an appointment as a teacher in the Upper School of the Ramallah Friends School. While on sabbatical in England from my work at Guilford, I visited her in the spring of '99.

I was struck anew by the continuing development. Now Ramallah had a supermarket! And museums emphasizing pride in Palestinian culture had been developed there and in Bethlehem. It was moving to see Palestinians able to celebrate their rich heritage unfettered by pre-Oslo Israeli restrictions.

The school was flourishing. Facilities were being renovated, and tuition money wasn't as hard to come by with the population growth in Ramallah and steady incomes from workers in the Palestinian Authority. Having merged administrations as a money-saving measure during the first Intifada, the school was now co-educational all the way through the grades, and teachers were being trained for an introduction of the International Baccalaureate program.

Beyond the vast improvements in the buildings and grounds of the school, I noticed another, less positive, sign of changes in Ramallah. While there during the summer of the first Intifada, I was told by many people that the energy of the uprising would translate into a different attitude about authority, and I certainly saw the truth of that in Maia's classes. She had told me how difficult discipline was in the school. Some students openly defied her and others, sometimes physically trying to intimidate teachers. When I taught in the early '70s, students rose by their seats when the teacher entered the room, standing at attention until they were asked to sit. Even when I was sitting in on Maia's classes, I saw no vestige of that old practice of respect.

Maia and I hiked through the valleys replete with spring flowers and peasant farmers plowing. On Easter Sunday, we watched the sunrise. On another day we traveled to Tel Aviv to tour Old Jaffa, a once thriving Arab city turned into an expensive artists' neighborhood of Tel Aviv. The Arabic architecture and old mosques were a reminder of what once was—and what many feared East Jerusalem might become under Israel's stated policy of "judaization" of the primarily Palestinian area.

My main reason for visiting Old Jaffa was to find the grave of Thomas Hodgkin, a British Quaker doctor in the 19th century famous for his study of the lymphatic system and other medical innovations. He was also noted for his critique of British policies impacting the First Nations people in Canada, which impacted his ability to advance in hospital administration in London. After being denied the leadership of Guy's Hospital, he committed to addressing the problem of cholera in North Africa and the Middle East, traveling with the financial and personal support of Sir Moses Montefiore, a prominent member of England's Jewish community.

In 1866, Hodgkin died in Jaffa of cholera. Montefiore paid for an obelisk to be erected over his grave in the cemetery behind the Church of Scotland Girls School. We found the grave in the rather unkempt graveyard. Hodgkin's obelisk, however, was in good shape. It might be noted that one other memorial to a person revered by Moses Montefiore was erected through his efforts: biblical Rachel's tomb in Bethlehem.

While in Ramallah visiting Maia, I also worked on arrangements for that summer's work trip. With Maia's assistance, it would prove to be far more expansive than any of our previous programs.

The cautious optimism we had heard from some in '97 had given way to full-blown hope for many in '99. Netanyahu and his avowed attempt to destroy the Oslo peace process had been replaced in Israel by Prime Minister Ehud Barak. There was something of an "Israeli Spring" in the works. Troops were being removed from Lebanon; new, critical scholarship about Israel's history was being encouraged; social contacts between Israelis and Palestinians were growing. There was a sense of encouragement I had seldom experienced before.

Meeting again with Yehezkel Landau, we heard his almost giddy excitement over prospects for peace. A Palestinian state in most of the West Bank and Gaza was a "done deal," he told us. "The various plans for how it might happen are in negotiators' desk drawers." A parent at the Friends School and descendant of one of the original families to settle Ramallah in the 1500s told us that a Palestinian state was imminent, but that it must be on one hundred percent of the occupied territories. Jean Zaru shared with us about her work with Sabeel and the impact of liberation theology on growing Palestinian confidence in the rightness of their cause. Adel Yahya, founder of the Palestinian Association for Cultural Exchange (PACE), led us on an archaeological tour and shared his vision of a booming tourism industry in Palestine.

But still there were signs that the Peaceable Kingdom had not quite arrived. Hanan Ashrawi, a Friends Girls School graduate, Palestinian spokeswoman at the Madrid peace talks and former first minister of education in Arafat's Palestinian Authority Cabinet, told us that the peace process was stalling. She gave a blistering critique of Oslo, saying that the Palestinians had been tricked into accepting the provisions of the accords—which favored Israel over the Palestinians. She was not shy about criticizing Arafat's government, either. In fact, she had resigned from her post as education minister because of corruption in the Palestinian Authority. She had gone on to form an independent organization to build the kind of democratic institutions a future Palestinian state would require.

Our meeting with a resident of Efrat, a Jewish settlement on the outskirts of Bethlehem, also offered caution. Efrat was established in 1983 on one hilltop, and already it was spreading over the adjoining hills. We were told that the land had been purchased fairly and legally from the neighboring Arab village and that relations with those neighbors were excellent. But he was clear that "this is our land." He was not pleased that a Palestinian woman from Ramallah had accompanied us on our visit to Efrat, and he was clearly impatient with her comments that challenged his rosy view of the settlement and Palestinian relations.

Our work at the school was also different from '97. Instead of chipping plaster and hauling dirt, we did a lot of painting, one day spiffing up seventy chairs from classrooms, and another time painting the playground equipment and classroom of the Friends Play Center in the Amari refugee camp in Ramallah. Violet Zaru, a founder of the play center for five-year-olds, told us that the program served more than fifty children from the camp who otherwise would have little opportunity for a nutritious meal, carefree play, and assurance that there were those outside the camp who cared for and loved them.

Joining us for some of the discussions in Ramallah were Jonathan and Sarah Malino, a faculty couple at Guilford College who were in Jerusalem for a philosophy conference. Jonathan, a non-congregational rabbi, was good friends with a Friends School parent who was also a philosopher and an administrator at the Palestinian Al-Quds University.

I also talked with former students, who revealed that the optimism about the peace process had led to new business relationships between Israelis and Palestinians. Ihsan, owner of an ice cream store, purchased his dairy supplies from a kibbutz, and there was free social exchange on mutual visits. Ameen, who ran a nursery business, got his plants from an Israeli source, and they, too, visited back and forth. Israelis were frequently in Ramallah to shop and eat at the growing number of fine restaurants—especially residents of Jerusalem, where growing ultra-Orthodox influence was stifling nightlife. One Israeli told me that he had moved from Jerusalem to the more secular Tel Aviv because "there's too much God in Jerusalem now!"

We left Ramallah that summer with the hope that peace was around the corner and that, perhaps, the next work trip would be to a sovereign state of Palestine.

Chapter 5: The Second Intifada, Part 1

Bill Clinton's last-ditch effort to broker a peace deal between the Palestinians and Israelis failed at Camp David in the waning months of his presidency in July 2000, and in spite of promises made to the Palestinians that they would not be blamed if the talks failed, they were. The myth of Arafat's rejection of Ehud Barak's "generous offer" of a Palestinian state gained traction, although it was later shown to be just that—a myth—by Arafat's willingness to negotiate at the follow-up conference in Taba in January of 2001. But it was Barak who left the table, hurrying back to Israel to try to salvage his campaign for re-election.

That disappointment and sense of betrayal further fueled Palestinian unrest as they saw Oslo deadlines come and go with no final status agreement, an accelerating spread of Jewish settlements in the occupied territories, and a growing right-wing movement in Israel to scuttle Oslo. As in '87, frustration created the kindling that needed a spark, and it was provided in September of 2000. Ariel Sharon, mounting a campaign to be prime minister of Israel, visited the Haram es-Sharif/Temple Mount complex in Jerusalem with an escort of more than 1,000 Israeli border police. The second Intifada began.

Initially, the fatalities and injuries were almost exclusively Palestinian as anger at Sharon's encroachment on the Muslim holy sites of the Al-Aqsa Mosque and Dome of the Rock led to stone throwing and demonstrations, with the inevitable IDF and border police response of rubber bullets, live ammunition, and tear gas. But within a few weeks there were Israeli casualties as well and a series of suicide bombings. Unlike the first Intifada, which was highly organized and overwhelmingly nonviolent in the early years, this one was spontaneous and became increasingly more deadly. Deaths and injuries mounted on both sides.

As we planned our summer of '01 work trip, we were confronted with the question of whether we should cancel the program as we had on previous occasions when there had been the threat of violence. The six confirmed participants—three Guilford students and three older adults—continued to want to go. And our program partners in Palestine and Israel encouraged us to come as an important accompaniment to those seeking a nonviolent response. They also urged us to come as witnesses to what was actually happening on the ground.

Following some serious prayer and reflection, we decided to proceed with the trip.

Our journey did not begin well. Our AirFrance flight had been cancelled from Paris to Tel Aviv, and nobody had informed us before we arrived at the airport. Jane worked her magic and got us a flight and overnight accommodations in Paris. While there, I was mugged on the subway and lost $1,500 of group money. It seemed like a bad omen.

Maia, who had remained in the Middle East a third year to work in Amman, Jordan, met us at the airport when we arrived in Tel Aviv and accompanied us to Ramallah. There, two Friends School students who would later attend Guilford College, and another who was already enrolled, met us at the Upper School campus and took us for a stroll through town to Rukab's ice cream store, now thoroughly remodeled and expanded. All on the streets greeted us pleasantly. A constant theme of our time during the visit was the deep gratitude shown to us for making the trip during such a trying time.

The two future Guilfordians joined us the next day on our first work assignment—four hours of clearing weeds and hauling dirt for future plantings of trees in an abandoned area of the Upper School (the former Boys School) campus. At lunch, as we sat on the veranda of Grant Hall chatting, we heard the pop-pop-pop of weapon fire nearby. Members of our group jumped at the sound and expressed their trepidation. The Palestinian students said not to worry. It was just the *shabaab* firing old bolt action rifles toward the settlement on Jabal Taweel, and the bullets wouldn't even reach the security fence around the settlement. Soon after we heard the rat-a-tat-tat of machine gun fire from the settlement in return, but by then the young boys had already run away. It was a cat and mouse game, and before our visit was over, we could tell which firing was Palestinian and which was Israeli.

In the afternoon of that first full day, we went on a tour with Adel Yahya of the Palestinian Association for Cultural Exchange (PACE). He first took us by the archaeological sites in Ramallah and El-Bireh that he was helping develop as part of the Palestinian tourism industry. A Ph.D. in Archaeology from the University of Pennsylvania, he had made great progress developing PACE until the Intifada broke out. Tourism had all but vanished.

After viewing the ruins of an ancient Byzantine church dedicated to the Holy Family and maintained by the neighboring mosque, we went to an area that was the scene of weekly clashes following Friday prayers. As further "cat and mouse" activity of the Intifada, Palestinians would gather on one side of the no man's land separating Ramallah/El-Bireh from the Israeli settlement of Bet-El, site also of the administrative headquarters of the Israeli occupation of the West Bank.

The area between Palestinian control and Israeli control was blackened by months of burning tires, Molotov cocktails, and conflict. The ground was littered with rubber bullets and tear gas canisters. As we viewed the burned-over district, an Israeli jeep came careening toward us and screeched to a halt. "You must leave here immediately," one of the soldiers told us. "There are Palestinian snipers on all the buildings, and you are in danger of being shot." Adel laughed and told us we had nothing to fear; there were no snipers. But we moved on anyway.

Our tour continued past homes of leaders in the Palestinian Authority and through the Christian village of Jifna and the mixed town of Bir Zeit. We saw numerous Israeli tanks and armored personnel carriers along the road. We also saw that all access roads from Palestinian villages to the main highway had been blocked by the IDF—some by ditches; some by enormous boulders; others by large concrete barricades. If villagers were to come to the larger cities for shopping, business, or school, they either had to walk through the open countryside or find circuitous routes by vehicle to the main highways. A normal journey of fifteen minutes had turned into a harrowing trial of several hours.

Following more working days cleaning and painting, as well as hospitality in the home of the Guilford student, we traveled to Jerusalem. The formerly fifteen-minute taxi trip now took much longer. A major checkpoint had been erected just outside the Qalandiya refugee camp on Ramallah's outskirts.

In Jerusalem, we tried to visit the Dome of the Rock and Al-Aqsa Mosque, but access was closed. We would learn later that even if the Haram es-Sharif/Temple Mount area had been open, non-Muslims were no longer being allowed access to the interior of the holy buildings.

Our main purpose for the trip, though, was to meet with Rabbi Arik Ascherman, a leader of Rabbis for Human Rights (RHR), in his West Jerusalem office. As we approached his building, we noticed posters on walls with his likeness on them above Hebrew text. When we asked Arik about them, he laughed and said, "They are flyers calling for my assassination; there is a price on my head for expressing sympathy for the Palestinians." RHR promoted human rights for all and opposed the settlements, olive tree destruction, home demolitions, and stereotyping that were in opposition to the social justice traditions of Judaism.

Members of our group with Rabbi Arik Ascherman of Rabbis for Human Rights. He is the tall one in the back row. Jane is on the left in the back row; Maia is second from the right in the back row.

Back in Ramallah at the school, Tamara, the Guilford student, stopped by to tell us that members of the youth wing of Hamas had ransacked a friend's graduation party, incensed that they were celebrating at such a time. Samer, one of the Friends School students assisting us, called to tell us there had been a suicide bomber in Tel Aviv and that clashes had broken out. His family had offered to take us all in if we were nervous, but we felt fine staying in our accommodations at the school.

After two days of work turning the former school gardener's home into a physical education facility, we met with Ghassan Khatib, a Palestinian political scientist and pollster. He explained why Oslo had failed and the Intifada erupted: after ten years of negotiations, there was no end in sight to the Israeli occupation.

Trips to Hebron and Wahat al-Salam/Neve Shalom (WSNS) interrupted work over the next few days. Only a few went to Hebron, as it was reported closed, and only Maia and a few other brave souls dared take a taxi there. At the Israeli peace community, we were given the tour by an Israeli Arab who shared with us that she had hated Israeli Jews before attending a peace camp one summer in the community. Now she was a resident. She also reported that an Israeli Jewish community was being planned near WSNS as a statement that not all were pleased with the integrated community.

Israeli soldiers outside the Ibrahimi Mosque in Hebron.

During another visit to Jerusalem, we joined in a demonstration on King George St. in West Jerusalem with Women in Black, a combined Israeli and Palestinian group protesting the occupation. About sixty people participated in the silent vigil. Hard right-wingers, many in their teens, held a counter-demonstration. Some of their signs read "End the Arab Occupation" and "Drive out the Arab Occupiers." Some of the members of Women in Black shared with us how the hate speech hurled at them during their demonstrations was taken very seriously, citing the hate speech that preceded Prime Minister Yitzhak Rabin's assassination in 1995 and the threats of violence against others in peace organizations.

There was more work back in Ramallah and more encounters with the Intifada. While shopping for the group one day, Jane and I came across a loud and large funeral procession for a *shaheed* (martyr) who had died of injuries sustained in a clash three weeks before. There was firing and shouting, but all greeted us with hellos and expressions of friendliness.

Another Palestinian political scientist, Ali Jarbawi, met with us and outlined in terms similar to others' descriptions how desperate current conditions were, the Israeli state of mind, and his view of possible outcomes.

Our work in Ramallah was mostly finished, and after Sunday worship with Ramallah Friends Meeting, we traveled to the Israeli Arab village of Ibillin and the Mar Elias Educational Trust. In addition to using the facilities as a home base for exploring the Upper Galilee and its biblical sites, we also did a work project at the Maryam Bawardi Kindergarten of the Mar Elias School, one day joined by Abuna Elias Chacour, the internationally known Melkite priest, peacemaker, and founder of the school. In his priest's robes, he helped us chip away at impossibly cemented tiles in the bathrooms.

That night, Abuna invited us to join him on the rooftop of his residence. He described how Israeli soldiers had killed one of the school's students the previous fall during demonstrations against land confiscation. Asel Asleh had attended a Seeds of Peace camp, was an advocate of nonviolence, and was simply sitting under an olive tree. "Arab/Jewish relations are now back to where they were fifty years ago," Abuna said. "We are not second or third-class citizens of the state; we are no-citizens."

On the way back to Ramallah by way of the Jordan Valley, we stopped at Kibbutz Tirat Zvi, home of the wife of an Israeli student at Guilford. While there, we learned of the 1937 founding of the kibbutz, a miraculous rain storm's halting the advance on the kibbutz by Iraqi regulars during the '48 war, and the kibbutz's good relations with Jordanian farmers across the river.

Back in Ramallah, we had occasion to take a walk with Mohammad, the Friends School teacher who was helping arrange our program, to visit his cousin. Her home had been hit by Israeli gunfire two nights before. We walked past the Palestinian governmental headquarters, the *Muqata'a*, and on to a grouping of houses and small shops on the outskirts of El-Bireh. Although there was no reason for the attack, an Israeli armored vehicle had lumbered into the area at 2:30 a.m., blasted the Palestinian checkpoint, fired a shell through a grocery store, and raked two houses with machine gun fire.

As we examined the damage—the broken windows, pock-marked limestone, shredded curtains, and punctured water tanks—Nadia, a 27-year old mother of three small children, came out of her blasted home, welcomed us, and even served us soft drinks. She then described the terror of the night attack: "We thought we were all going to die. Bullets raked our bedroom for half an hour as my husband and I huddled with our children on the floor, assuming we would be killed. When we miraculously survived and began cleaning up our house, what do you think we found engraved on the bullet casings? 'Made in USA.' And you call us the terrorists!"

An Israeli artillery shell went through the grocery store neighboring Nadia's home.

All we could do was listen, express our sympathy, and take it in. Deeply shaken, we left to attend a planned supper at a Ramallah restaurant. On the way, we shared among ourselves how we had learned in discussions with Khatib, Jarbawi, and Abuna Chacour how American military aid to Israel comes out to $20 per year for each man, woman, and child in the U.S. We determined to contribute $20 apiece, along with other funds, to aid in the rebuilding of Nadia's home. Mohammad delivered the money to her the next day.

After supper, two of the Friends School students met with us back at Grant Hall and shared their insights into the situation: Prime Minister Barak's "generous offer" was for only a portion of the historical British Mandate Palestine comprising the West Bank and Gaza, even after Palestinians overwhelmingly recognized Israel on seventy-eight percent of the Palestinians' historical homeland. They went on to say that it had been a tragic mistake for Palestinians to use violence and gunfire after the second Intifada broke out. It discouraged mass demonstrations for fear of crossfire—and besides, "Palestinian guns go 'tic-tic-tic,' while Israel responds with machine guns."

As our time in Ramallah grew short, we continued to wonder about Nadia and her family. How were they coping with the trauma of the night invasion? Were they able to repair their home? Did they view our donation as "blood money"? We feared the latter, as we didn't hear anything from her by way of her cousin Mohammad. But during a supper at Mohammad's home, a sumptuous feast that he and his wife prepared for us, the phone rang. It was Nadia, asking if "the Americans" were there. She wanted to visit, introduce us to her family, and thank us.

It wasn't long before Nadia, her husband, and their three small children arrived. We chatted happily, with no sign of the anger Nadia first expressed to us. She even apologized for venting. We said that we certainly understood, given the circumstances. And then the conservative, covered Muslim woman asked, "Are Quakers Christians?"

Jane gave me a stern look, knowing that I could go on for hours discussing the various branches of Friends, the debates among some about whether Quakerism is necessarily Christian and whether one could be called a Quaker without a thoroughly Christian theology. "Just say yes, Max," she said. "Yes," I said.

"I thought so," Nadia replied. "But I didn't want to offend." And then this Muslim woman, whose family had very nearly been killed by bullets manufactured in a so-called Christian nation, began pulling little trinkets out of a bag to give us as tokens of her appreciation: olive wood crosses and Jerusalem cross key chains. We were in tears.

On July 29, *Tisha B'Av* on the Jewish calendar—the commemoration of the destruction of the Jerusalem temple—we visited the Palestine Media Center and the office of Yasser Abed Rabbo, the former PLO guerrilla and press secretary for Yasser Arafat. Now an advocate for peace and a two-state solution, he talked with us as he divided his attention between us and the expected drama of a group of radical Jews who were driving a flatbed truck into Jerusalem with the "cornerstone" for the third temple. It was an annual symbolic display of the hope among some Jews and Christian Zionists that the Muslim holy sites of the Dome of the Rock and Al-Aqsa Mosque would be replaced by the temple.

Following that visit, we returned to the Friends School for another meeting with a leading Palestinian political figure. Fresh from participation in a nonviolent demonstration at the Qalandiya checkpoint, Marwan Barghouti met with us, accompanied by three well-armed bodyguards. He apologized for the armed presence in a Quaker space, but explained that he was Israel's number-one target for assassination.

Although he had spent five months in an Israeli prison, during which time he had been kept in isolation and tortured, and later exiled before the Oslo Accords allowed him to return, Barghouti expressed his support for a two-state solution. "A solution to our situation requires recognition of each other. I supported Oslo, and I meet with Israelis and members of the Knesset. It's time to understand how to live together. Israel wants security, but they are not committed to a peace process. Only a just peace will bring their security."

One of the students asked whether he feared assassination, and he replied, "Israel has killed fifty-seven of my friends thus far, including those actively working for peace. But, no, I am not concerned. Why would they actually try to kill me? I'm a moderate. If they take people like me out, who will they negotiate with?"

Shortly after we returned to the States, we learned that an Israeli Apache attack helicopter had targeted Barghouti's car convoy. He jumped out just before the rockets hit. Two of his bodyguards were killed. In an invasion of Ramallah by the IDF early in 2002, he was arrested and imprisoned.

We finished work the next day, accompanied to the end by the two students who would later attend Guilford. Their care for us and attention to the unfolding events around us continued to impress us, as did their maturity, intelligence, and humor. Sitting on a bulldozer that was being used on another project at the school, Basil commented, "This is symbolic of the Palestinian situation: we never solve our problems; we just push them around!" On another occasion, when Samer invited us to his home on the edge of town, he said, "Don't worry about coming out that far; there are two tall buildings between us and the fighting!"

On our last full day in Ramallah, we learned that eight Palestinians had been killed in Nablus when an Apache helicopter fired two rockets into the third-floor window of an office building, targeting two people. Four others in the office were killed, as were two boys on the street below, waiting to be picked up from a summer camp. Two others had been killed in Gaza. The events sparked an immediate strike throughout the West Bank, and all stores and restaurants closed. We made do for supper with the leftovers we had.

We could feel the tension building and noticed that several in the streets had weapons—even bows and arrows. Several of the students who helped us during our work camp came to the school that evening to talk with us. All expressed fear that desperate Palestinians would do something to provoke Israel—and that it was precisely what Israel was hoping, so there could be a justification for even more drastic measures against the Palestinians. The students even displayed a grudging admiration for how cleverly Israel had pulled off proclaiming the myth that there was no cycle of violence—only Palestinian violence and limited, restrained Israeli action in self-defense, as one aide to Prime Minister Sharon had recently stated. "If only the Palestinian Authority could be so bright," they said.

The next day, amid tears of good-byes, we left Ramallah and the ongoing developments of the second Intifada. When we returned safely to the States after the trip, we were often asked, "Were you ever in danger? Weren't you frightened?" My response was usually, "Oh, no. We didn't go anywhere as dangerous as Paris!"

Chapter 6: The Second Intifada, Part 2

Only a month after we returned from the 2001 work trip, the attacks of September 11 occurred. I learned about the first plane hitting the World Trade Center in New York as I left my early morning class at Guilford—a Quakerism class that was studying the Book of Revelation.

I dashed over to the student center to see how students were reacting and to catch the news on the big screen TV. As I entered the lobby, the first person I saw was Tamara, a student from the Ramallah Friends School. "Oh, please God, don't let it be Palestinians!" she remarked.

I got to the TV room just in time to see the second plane hit the Twin Towers.

That afternoon, I helped organize a meeting for worship for the campus so that the community could begin processing the unbelievable tragedy together. Out of the silence of the Quaker-style meeting, students, faculty, and staff shared their grief and spoke the names of those they were worried about.

As I exited the meeting for worship, I saw that the local media were assembled—as they often were at the college following such major events. They knew that reaction at a Quaker institution would somehow be different. A TV reporter who knew me and my association with the Middle East approached and asked, "What do you think of the reports saying that Palestinians are dancing on their rooftops and in the streets in celebration of these attacks?"

I told her that I had heard no such reports, but that she could ask a Palestinian herself, and I summoned Haya who had been at the worship and was standing nearby. "Haya," I said, "This reporter says that Palestinians are celebrating the attacks. Do you know anything about it?" "No," Haya replied, "But let me call my mother back home."

With that, Haya got on her cell phone, called her mother, and asked if Palestinians were in the streets celebrating. Her mother told her to wait a minute, went outside, and came back to report: "No."

With growing clamor for war in the United States, and the continued circulation of the myth of Palestinian celebration over the attacks, I returned to the Middle East the following summer. This time it wasn't with a work trip to the Friends School, or even in the company of Jane. Though I would meet her in Ramallah for Haya's wedding, most of my time would be spent with a study group sponsored by the American Friends Service Committee.

The AFSC had published two major works about the Israeli/Arab conflict, *Search for Peace in the Middle East* and *A Compassionate Peace*. They were planning a third, and this study group was to spend three weeks in the region gathering information that a small writing group would turn into a book. The group consisted largely of international Quakers with particular expertise in the situation. There were directors of peace and conflict studies programs at Quaker colleges; a black Quaker from South Africa; an African-American professor; AFSC representatives from Philadelphia, Washington, D.C., and the Middle East; a Palestinian Quaker; an internationally known journalist and author who specialized in the Middle East; a former AFSC legal aid staffer in Jerusalem; a Jewish Quaker activist; an Earlham alumna who had gone on to write the ground-breaking *One Land, Two Peoples: The Conflict over Palestine*. And me.

We first gathered in Amman, Jordan, where we met with Shaher Bak, Deputy Foreign Minister. He emphasized that the violence of the Intifada would decrease if Israel and the Palestinians began negotiations, but the talks must include ending the occupation and, eventually, negotiating about the right of return for Palestinian refugees. While most of the conversation was about Palestine/Israel, he did comment on the growing concern in the region that the Bush administration was talking about invading Iraq. "The consequences would be a disaster," he emphasized. "Yes, Saddam's regime is brutal, but how many such regimes are there in the world? Must the U.S. send forces to all of them?"

Our meeting with Bak was followed by another meeting in the Foreign Ministry—with Marouf al-Bakhit, a former army general who was working as a peace coordinator. He spoke of his involvement with the "Arab Initiative," a recent peace plan approved by twenty-two Arab states (including Iraq). It recognized Israel's need for security and guaranteed it in return for an end to the occupation and flexibility on the refugee issue. "The Arab states want an historic reconciliation. Israel cannot defeat a people," he told us.

In discussions with Mustafah Hamameh, a professor at the University of Jordan's Institute for Strategic Studies, we heard deep pessimism about the situation between Israel and the Palestinians. "This is the most desperate it has been in the forty-nine years I have been aware of the issues," he told us. "All the arguments coming out of Israel are the old colonial ones. The Palestinians are now so angry that they are rejecting a two-state solution and are returning to asking for all of historical Palestine. And Israel is not interested in regional cooperation; they imagine themselves to be somewhere between New York and London. Palestinian talk about nonviolence is now out; suicide bombings have raised awareness of the Palestinians. Only the U.S. or far-sighted Israelis can push a peace process forward now."

On our second day in Amman, we met with Prince Hassan at a royal palace. He had been the Crown Prince but was passed over for Abdullah II following King Hussein's death in 1999. With typical Bedouin hospitality, he received us with thick coffee served by an attendant in a red *keffieyeh* decked out in robes with a dagger and bullets in his belt. The prince spoke of his own intellectual pursuits in history and archaeology, displaying a keen knowledge about Christian messianic theology and the battle of Armageddon. "It is surreal," he told us. Hassan also spoke positively about the Arab Initiative and told of his own conversations with Jewish musician Yehudi Menuhin about holding a parliament of world cultures. "Sadly, though," he said, "the West sees the Arab world as important only for buying weapons and exporting oil."

Next we met with former Foreign Minister Kamel Abu Jaber. In contrast to Prince Hassan's good humor and laidback demeanor, Abu Jaber expressed deep anger over the West's and the United States' abandonment of the Arab world. "The whole Arab world feels targeted, helpless, friendless. The Americans are lovely people, but the government has lurched so far to the right—what happened to it?" He was pessimistic and felt hopeless. He also spoke of his anger with Israel and its actions, citing past good relations between Jews and Arabs. "Israel has stolen our hearts and minds and directed our energies toward this God-forsaken conflict. Instead of dreaming about cooperation with Israel to improve the region, young people now dream of becoming martyrs." Although his feelings about the West were apparent, he did share how deeply grateful he was for his childhood education at the Bishop's School under a Quaker headmaster, James Sutton.

A meeting with staff of the United Nations Relief and Works Agency (UNRWA) introduced us to both the plight and aspirations of Palestinian refugees. Schools and health centers operated by UNRWA served a population that made up almost one-half of Jordan's citizens—only seventeen percent of whom lived in camps. Frustration was building, we were told, owing to the international community's inability to address the refugee situation. But if Israel accepted responsibility for what happened to the Palestinian refugees, the general sentiment seemed to be, then there could be many possible accommodations to the refugee situation, including compensation, remaining where refugees had settled, moving to the West Bank, and limited physical return to the state of Israel.

We visited the Baq'a refugee camp outside Amman and met with an elderly leader of the community—a double refugee from '48 and '67. Dignified and proud, he showed no anger, denounced terrorism, and desired a Middle East that was an "oasis of peace" with security for all. He didn't want an armed struggle, but he wanted United Nations resolutions on the right of return to be implemented. Touring one immaculate though cramped camp home, we met a proud, defiant young mother. Pointing to a map showing the destroyed Palestinian villages following the '48 war, she said, "We would return to our homes in Palestine, even if this home became a palace!"

Following our time in Amman, we divided into three smaller groups to visit Lebanon, Syria, and Egypt. I chose to go to Egypt, and five of us flew off to Cairo.

Our first conversation in Egypt was with Mukhtar el-Fayoumi, a former military officer and arms control expert. He spoke of how important understanding Islam is—and how uninformed so many in the West are about it. "Islam is a unified way of life. It isn't the 'terrorism' it is painted to be. Nowhere in the Qur'an are we told to 'kill the Jews.' We, too, are the victims of terrorism." He went on to tell us that the U.S. had lost its credibility as a broker in the Israeli-Palestinian crisis. "We've been following the American lead for the past ten years, but there has been no improvement." Speaking of the billions of dollars in annual aid the U.S. sends to Egypt as a result of the peace treaty with Israel, he told us it was not a benefit to the general population. The money is for purchasing U.S. military equipment—and for providing security for the U.S. El-Fayoumi also echoed a persistent theme we had heard in Jordan: Israel is paranoid about security and rejects any peace initiative that doesn't guarantee security. "But where in the world is there a one hundred percent absence of violence? Can I guarantee your safety here in Cairo?"

With the director of the Al-Ahram Center for Strategic Studies, Abdel Monem Said Aly, we heard an exposition of what he saw as the only solution to the conflict: two states defined by the pre-'67 borders, the "Clinton Parameters" concerning the borders of Jerusalem, and acknowledgment of the principle of the right of return—but with sensitivity to Israel's demographic concerns. "The West must tell Palestinians that it understands their struggle, but 'You don't have to blow people up!' And it must tell Israel that it understands Jewish and Israeli suffering, but 'You live in this region, and when you came to this region, you found people here.' We must change the definition of 'victory' so both sides can achieve their national objectives: for Israel, security; for Palestinians, their own state." He went on to express deep concern that the longer the conflict went on without resolution, the stronger Islamic fundamentalism would become, and the issues, once seen as secular, would become religious.

We then met with Foreign Minister Ahmed Mahr el-Sayed. He viewed Israel as the last colonial power. "Most people in the world have been liberated, but here Israel uses force to quell the normal liberation struggle of a people. In turn, the people use means that are reprehensible. Certainly Israel will not disappear, but neither will the Palestinians. They are condemned to live together." Commenting on the failure at Camp David in 2000, he said that all sides made mistakes, including the U.S. for rushing the process. "Now," he said, "Israel has two goals: destroy the Oslo process and delegitimize Arafat." And he, too, remarked on the U.S. plan to invade Iraq. "It would be foolish for the U.S. to do it. We don't like Saddam, but if he is gotten rid of, something worse could replace him. Beyond the devastation this could cause in Iraq, there would be repercussions in the Arab world: a feeling that Islam is under attack by the West; moderate regimes would be at risk; Kurdish, Shi'ite, and Sunni divisions would be exacerbated. Saddam is contained, and the U.S. would make a serious mistake in attacking." He concluded his talk with us by citing both the Qur'an, "If you kill one person, you are killing all of humanity," and the Bible, "Do unto others as you would have them do unto you."

Taking a break from the intense discussions, we visited the pyramids, and later, I walked along the Nile alone, marveling at the historic river and the fully covered women sculling on the water. I also marveled at the traffic on the multi-laned Cairo streets and finally built up the courage to attempt a crossing, assured by locals that the careening cars would, in fact, part for me. They were right, and I developed an understanding of why Moses was able miraculously to part the waters of the sea on his escape with the Hebrew people from Egypt.

Back in meetings, we talked with a representative of the British Embassy who told us that much harder statements are made in private to Prime Minister Sharon of Israel than they are in public. She also told us that the U.K. was hoping for a balanced statement from President Bush in the anticipated U.S. plan for the region.

At the Ford Foundation, we met with staff who had Ramallah Friends School connections through family who had attended. They encouraged Quakers to be a moral voice in the conflict (echoing what I had heard before from Palestinian attorney Jonathan Kuttab). "Your voice is needed to counter the right-wing Christians," they said. "The conflict has made routine human rights violations banal and set human rights work back years."

At the American University of Cairo, we met with Sa'ad Ibrahim, a human rights activist and former PLO fighter who had joined the *fedayeen* in the "romantic" '60s. Escaping Amman after Black September, he began to see the same atrocities perpetrated by the PLO as by the Israeli oppressors. It led to his gradual conversion to the idea of peace. For eleven years he had been part of an Arab/Israeli peace initiative, "Search for Common Ground," but since the outbreak of the Intifada and 9/11, the group had not met. The moderates in power on all sides were dragging their feet on a resolution, and meanwhile extremists were gaining the upper hand. "Occupation and suicide bombings are both cardinal violations of human rights. The U.S. must condemn the bombings but also the cause of the bombings: the occupation—that, or tell the Palestinians how to resist! A new, nonviolent Intifada in the spirit of the first one needs to arise." He also urged Quakers to promote active nonviolent resistance.

In a meeting at the South African Embassy, we were told that South Africa could not be a broker in peace talks between Israel and the Palestinians, as Israel didn't trust South Africa's previous African National Congress' relations with the Palestinians. "But we recognize the existence of two states and support a political settlement through dialogue. Violence and counter-violence are counterproductive. South Africa is now a government, not a liberation movement. We condemn the suicide bombers and the force used by Israel. We are trying to be balanced."

And with that, our time in Egypt was over, and we returned to Jordan.

As the various groups reported on their experiences back at the hotel in Amman, we learned that there had been another suicide bombing on a Jerusalem bus, killing nineteen. We knew there would be reprisals, and we wondered how it would affect our plans as we prepared to travel to the West Bank and Israel. Jean Zaru, the lone Palestinian in our delegation, knew what it meant for her, and she left early for the bridge crossing into occupied territory. We followed later.

It took our international group an hour to be processed by the Jordanians before we took a bus across the Jordan River on the King Hussein/Allenby Bridge. It brought to mind the old spiritual, "Michael, Row the Boat Ashore," though the Jordan River was anything but "chilly and cold" or "deep and wide." The mere trickle was muddy, narrow, and reedy. And on the other side was anything but "milk and honey."

While Jean waited outside in the heat with other Palestinians, we internationals were being processed in an air-conditioned terminal by Israeli soldiers and border control. Two in the group were singled out for intense questioning about the purpose of our visit while our luggage was being screened by security. We were held in suspense for more than four hours, during which time even more Israeli officials got involved and discussed our purposes. Jean finally took a taxi herself to travel on to Jerusalem.

While we continued to wait, we chatted with some of the Palestinians waiting in long lines to gain permission to enter the West Bank. One who was from Washington state told us of his difficult journey to visit his sick mother in Jerusalem. Turned back with his family at the Tel Aviv airport, they flew to Frankfurt and purchased tickets to Amman and had new documents sent to them from America. Their trip had begun on June 8; it was now June 19. After hours of waiting, calls to the U.S. Embassy, and many more tears, he and his family were sent back to Amman.

Finally, feeling a bit guilty, we were given permission to pass through security and continue our journey to Jerusalem. We learned later that it was only through the intervention of Naomi Chazan, a member of Israel's Knesset with whom we were to meet later, that we gained entrance. Even at that, we missed our bus and had to take taxis to our accommodations, the YWCA in East Jerusalem.

After getting settled at the Y, we walked to the Jerusalem Hotel outside Damascus Gate for supper. There we met with attorney Jonathan Kuttab—who once again emphasized that Quakers should be prophetic rather than worry about being effective. He went on to say that the only strategy that would work for Palestinians against the Israeli occupation would be well-organized, nonviolent resistance.

Our first full day in the West Bank was a lesson in the growing impact of the Intifada. Our plan was to visit Bethlehem, but it was closed. Instead, we headed to Hebron, also reportedly closed, but we decided to take our chances. Our bus had yellow Jerusalem license plates, necessary in Israel's segregated road system to travel on the "settler roads" in the West Bank. However, because our bus had a Palestinian driver, we were turned back at the Israeli checkpoint outside Bethlehem near the Gilo settlement. As with other Arab drivers, however, he knew how to circumvent Israeli checkpoints and took us on a long, circuitous route through Palestinian villages and valleys west and south of Jerusalem and back onto the settler road just past the checkpoint.

We arrived in Hebron and sought access to the Old City by way of the Jewish settlement of Kiryat Arba. Security there refused our entry until the two ethnically Jewish members of our Quaker group talked to the guard. We were allowed in, passing through the settlement on our way to "H1," the eighty percent of the Palestinian city of 120,000 that Palestinians were free to access. "H2" was the twenty percent designated for the few hundred settlers who had taken up residence in the old market area.

The once thriving market area was like a ghost town. Settlers had built houses on top of the Palestinian shops and expanded their presence, often burrowing down into the shops below. There were wire mesh screens over the streets to guard against the rocks and garbage thrown by the settlers. We went to the Christian Peacemaker Teams apartment, and there was Kathy again—the CPT member who had guided us through the city in '97.

After meeting with her and hearing the description of the growing desperation of the Palestinian population, we walked back to the bus. There we saw Israeli soldiers roughing up a Palestinian boy, and several in the group started photographing the action. The soldiers didn't stop the picture-taking, but they didn't stop beating the boy, either. We didn't want to leave for our next appointment while the boy was being pummeled, but Kathy said she would remain behind, and we reluctantly drove away. As we did, we saw that the soldiers let the boy go.

We almost weren't allowed out of the city at the next Israeli checkpoint. The soldiers said they'd have to clear it with their superiors. While waiting, we chatted with the teenage soldiers. They confided in us that they had been in the military for almost three years already and couldn't wait to get out. And when they did, they told us, they were heading straight for South America!

Finally allowed out of Hebron, we went on to Dura, a Palestinian village in the hills of the southern West Bank. We could see the Mediterranean shimmering in the distance. Like most Palestinian towns, it had been completely cut off from the main road by boulders placed at all access points by the IDF. The bus had to park along the highway, and like other villagers, we walked over the barricades to the other side, hailing a taxi to take us on to the village. While crossing over, we saw women carrying enormous bundles from shopping and some men actually carrying stoves and refrigerators on their backs.

In the village, we met with a fiery journalist, Khalid Amayyeh, under house arrest by Israel. He was not in favor of a two-state solution but rather one secular, democratic state for all. "If the settlers want to stay; let them," he said. "They love this land just as we do. We can live together." But he warned of the growing influence of settler disciples of Rabbi Abraham Isaac Kook. "They are advocates of a 'Greater Israel' and believe that the Messiah will not come until there is major bloodshed. Politicians in the U.S. are blind to the looming danger of these extremists." He mentioned a conference being held that day in Jerusalem at which such extremists were calling for "Arab transfer" and "purity" in Israel. "Such things are driving Palestinians to such desperation that they are willing to blow themselves up." He advocated for a nonviolent alternative in resistance but said that a nonviolent strategy, not reciprocated by Israel, would be short-lived. "If the world assures Palestinians that they will not be eliminated by Israel, then a nonviolent strategy could develop."

The next day, I left the group for a time to join Jane in the wedding celebration for Haya in her village outside of Ramallah. Used to the easy transportation between Jerusalem and Ramallah before the second Intifada, I was not prepared for the odyssey before me. It took two separate taxis to traverse the two new checkpoints between the cities. All passengers had to get out at each checkpoint, walk through, and get new transportation on the other side. Goods had to be unloaded, hauled across the checkpoint, and loaded onto another truck. I learned later from my former student Ihsan that it had effectively ended his ice cream business outside of Ramallah.

At the third checkpoint, Qalandiya, I asked how I might get to Deir Dibwan, the village where the wedding would take place. I was told it was not possible; it, too, had been cut off, and the only access from Qalandiya was a settler road. However, I negotiated with a taxi driver who was willing, for an exorbitant fee, to risk driving on the forbidden roadway and drop me off at the blocked entrance to the village.

It was a mad-dash trip, but we made it to the cut-off access road. I walked the remaining two miles to Haya's home, learning later from attendees of the wedding that villagers had thought I was a settler wandering through town.

Happily reunited with Jane and enjoying the lavish hospitality of Haya's family, we joined in the festivities—a joyous celebration of defiance and observation of Palestinian traditions and the beginning of Haya's new life with her husband.

After the wedding, Jane joined me for a day in Jerusalem while I rejoined the group and before she continued her trip with a planned visit to Ramallah. To get to Jerusalem, however, with Deir Dibwan closed off, we had to hire an internal taxi to drive through olive groves, over pastures, around boulders and across dry *wadis*, finally jumping a final embankment and landing on the major highway to Jerusalem.

Back with the AFSC group, we met with Mahdi Abdul Hadi, the director of the Palestinian Academic Society for the Study of International Affairs (PASSIA), a Palestinian think tank funded by USAid. He showed us maps of the West Bank, divided into areas under Palestinian, Israeli, and joint control as dictated by the Oslo Accords. They displayed in stark detail how much of the West Bank and Gaza were still controlled by Israel, the strategic location of the spreading Israeli settlements, and the unlikely possibility that a viable Palestinian state could be created out of such a fragmented whole. "We are now living in an apartheid/bi-national state. Palestinians are living a catastrophe, and Israelis are living a nightmare."

Following Abdul Hadi's talk, we heard from a Muslim cleric on the PASSIA staff. He shared how central Jerusalem is in Islam but that Arab East Jerusalem was becoming a "dead city" as Israel continued to "judaize" it. The history of the city, though, was of Jewish, Christian, and Muslim cooperation—with the exception of the Crusaders, who slaughtered Jews, Muslims, and Arab Christians alike. He lamented the fact that Christians around the world watched Israel's siege of the Church of the Nativity early in the second Intifada and did nothing, and he cited the loss of Muslim control of the Ibrahimi Mosque in Hebron following the Goldstein massacre as reason to oppose sharing the Haram es-Sharif/Temple Mount with Jews. His vision for Jerusalem was two capitals, two flags, and two municipalities.

The reality of growing apartheid and "judaization" was further emphasized later at a meeting with Michael Warschawsky in West Jerusalem at the Alternative Information Center. He took us on a tour of the settlements around Jerusalem and described how these settlements were planned to maximize Jewish population in Jerusalem and the West Bank and prevent any viable Palestinian entity. There are different rules for Arabs and Jews, he emphasized, all for the purpose of encouraging "voluntary transfer" of Palestinians out of the city. One of the most disturbing scenes on the tour was seeing how Bedouins had been displaced from their traditional grazing lands around Jerusalem and forced into residences in metal cargo containers on the city dump.

At a subsequent meeting with a scholar from Birzeit University, Albert Aghazarian, we were told how the situation was leading to aberrant behavior among Palestinians: "When I hear about a suicide bombing, I feel happy. This is not how I am supposed to feel. If we got a real peace deal, all would rise up against the suicide bombers and say it is an aberration and must stop." Speaking of the U.S. role as a broker, he said, "America has two souls: one that destroyed the Indians and one represented by the Quakers. Right now the former is prevailing."

That evening, we traveled to Tel Aviv and a secretive meeting with Uri Avnery, an Israeli who had fought in the '48 war for Israel but had gone on to help found *Gush Shalom*, the Israeli peace bloc, and become, as he put it, the hard core of the Israeli peace movement. We met secretly, as he was a hated and hunted man in Israel. He spoke with us of his hope for coexistence in peace with the Palestinians and detailed his critique of the failed Camp David meetings, Arafat's agreements at Taba, and Ehud Barak's duplicitous nature. "What he offered the Palestinians was an annexation of one-fifth of the West Bank and the demand that they capitulate on water resources, settlements, and refugees. Barak lived one hundred yards from Arafat at Camp David and never once spoke to him directly." As with other speakers of the day, he believed that Ariel Sharon was trying to complete the work of the 1948 war, but Palestinians were not capitulating, leading to intense Israeli anger.

The next day our group met with Moshe Maoz, director of the Truman Institute for Peace at Hebrew University, and Deputy Speaker of the Knesset, Naomi Chazan. She told us how she managed to get us through security at the Jordan River. Contacted by the border police, she was asked if she knew the people in our group. She had the list AFSC had sent her and read off the names. When the police asked her if the names were real, she responded, "Who would make up names like those?"

Both Chazan and Maoz were very critical of Israeli policies while decrying the violence of the Intifada. "I was born here and have been through five wars, but this is the worst I have seen it," Maoz said. "Sixty percent on both sides advocate living together, while eighty percent on both sides support violence! We lack leadership." Disappointed that Israel did not embrace the Arab Initiative for peace, he stated that it was because of Israel's fear of the right of return, even though the initiative was actually flexible on that issue. "There is no trust on either side," he claimed. "Even Israeli academics are distrustful of the Palestinians. They believe they don't want *salaam* (peace) but salami—a piece by piece takeover of all of historical Palestine."

Chazan shared how she had friends who had lost children in the violence and how angry they were with her for her liberal views on peace with the Palestinians. Both societies, she believed, were traumatized, and under such circumstances they do terrible things. "Suicide bombers are obscene and a gross violation of human rights. Israel's F-16s, Apache helicopters, and cutting off humanitarian supplies are cruel, too, and a violation of human rights. There is no military solution; Israel will not surrender, and there is no stopping Palestinian nationalism." She anticipated that the current "Operation Defensive Shield" by Israel would be a re-occupation of the Palestinian territories and the development of a South African-style apartheid. "We suffer," she went on to say, "from the fact that there are two narratives of the history and experience here that are both true—but don't meet." With Maoz, Chazan saw the only answer as a return to a two-state solution on pre-'67 borders, dismantling the settlements, making

Jerusalem the capital for two states, and negotiating trade-offs on the right of return of refugees.

Later we met with Gadi Golan, Assistant Foreign Minister for Religious Affairs. He expressed his consternation that all of Israel's military might had not been able to stop the Intifada. To a group of Quakers he actually said, "Our overwhelming might has not been able to stop this. What can we do?" When we mentioned that addressing human rights issues and the legitimate concerns of the Palestinians might alleviate matters, he admitted to the suffering of the Palestinian people, but he went on to say that it was justified in order to protect the Jewish people.

Meeting with Azmi Bishara, an Arab member of the Knesset, we heard of the measures being taken against him even as a citizen of Israel and elected member of the Israeli parliament. He, too, noted how Israeli force was not working against the Palestinians and shared Golan's and others' pessimism about any resolution in the near future. For Bishara, though, there was only one way forward: some sort of viable Palestinian state.

Following these meetings, I noted in my journal that I had begun taking Larium, an anti-malarial drug, in preparation for a trip to Kenya that would immediately follow my time in the Middle East. The medication came with a warning that it had a side-effect of producing anxiety. I wrote that taking it in the middle of such a trip might just neutralize that effect.

As we traveled on to Gaza, I was surprised by how much bigger and more prosperous Gaza City was than I remembered—and how lovely our accommodations were in a hotel near the sea. But any notion of normalcy had already been curtailed when we passed through security at the Gaza border and noticed that there were no Palestinian workers being allowed into Israel any more. Our first meetings further cured us of any thoughts of normalcy.

Talking with the staff of a human rights organization, we were told of egregious violations by Israel of the Geneva Conventions on human rights. "Israel gets by with it, however," we were told, "by claiming they are at war." The staff described the effects of the trauma of attacks on Gaza. Children, especially, were being victimized. Nightmares, bed-wetting, and pictures drawn by kindergarteners of fire raining down from the sky were some of the indicators.

We took a tour of some of the refugee camps and quickly realized how limited any prosperity was in Gaza. We passed a number of bombed out buildings left over from Israel's most recent invasion. Near the border with Israel, we saw IDF tanks rumbling along near fields that farmers continued to cultivate.

That night at the hotel, we spent two hours processing the trip thus far and agonizing over how to prepare a balanced report while capturing the dire nature of the conflict and the impending humanitarian crisis. In the middle of our deliberations, we paused in amazement to hear President Bush deliver his speech on a Middle East peace plan. Amid the strategically placed boos and hisses from the group, we did hear him say, "Israel's occupation that began in 1967 must end." Faint hope?

At our first stop the next day—the United Nations office of the special coordinator for the Middle East peace process—we heard a more sophisticated critique than boos and hisses. While positive about the call to end settlement expansion, encouragement for reforms, ending the '67 occupation, and holding Palestinian elections, they saw that the onus had been placed on the Palestinians to take certain actions before Israel would have to do anything.

"The current trajectory is very dangerous," we were told. "If things continue as they are, it will only encourage Islamist and radical forces." However, one of the groups typically associated with those forces, Hamas, was described to us as much more than the "terrorist organization" Israel and the United States define it to be. Encouraged in its development by Israel as a counterweight to the PLO during the first Intifada, Hamas was, indeed, allied with the Muslim Brotherhood, but the vast majority of its activity was in providing social services to the people of Gaza, winning it great loyalty among the population.

Returning to Jerusalem, I finally got through by phone to Jane in Ramallah. The day after she arrived at the home of old friends near the Friends School, the Israeli army invaded Ramallah and put the city under a strict curfew. Electricity was cut off, and residents were allowed out to shop for four hours only every few days. Tanks and armored vehicles stood outside the house; snipers were in the trees and tall buildings. But she told me, "It's more boring than dangerous."

Our group's next meeting was with Sari Nusseibeh, president of Al-Quds University and the PLO representative for Jerusalem. He described himself as "not a nationalist." He preferred being given Israeli citizenship and full equal rights—something that he admitted would eventually lead to a change in the nation in favor of Palestinians. He had been one of the signers of a full-page ad in the paper calling for an end to the suicide bombings, not on moral grounds but on the grounds that they were counterproductive. He favored massive, nonviolent resistance.

Another bus trip took us to Tel Aviv University and a meeting with Yossi Alpher at the Jaffee Center for Strategic Studies. He was the first we heard to advocate for the building of a fence proposed by the Sharon government to separate Israel from the Palestinian West Bank—but in conjunction with dismantling the settlements. "The best we can hope for now," he told us, "is a divorce—and probably a messy divorce."

The next speaker was the director of the center, Shai Feldman. He felt that the real strategic issue was a demographic one. "By the end of the decade," he said, "Jews will be a minority west of the Jordan River." He was followed by Tanya Reinhardt, a professor of literature and media at the university. She shared how she recognized at the outset of the Oslo Accords that it was institutionalized apartheid. She encouraged boycotting all Israeli goods in the United States—not only those produced in the settlements.

On up the coast to Haifa, we met with a professor at Haifa University, the author of *Original Sins*. He saw two signs of hope. The first was that continuing hardship might force Israel to compromise. Tourism was being affected, and the economy was suffering. The second was military opposition to continued engagement. Troops trained for disciplined tank warfare against armies were joy-riding in tanks through Palestinian cities.

In the Israeli Arab city of Umm il-Fahim, we met with the mayor and heard of the many laws in Israel that discriminate against the twenty-five perent of the population who are non-Jews. Among the laws that adversely affect the residents of the city are those that restrict building permits and land ownership. As a result, the city was growing up, not out, and it was becoming far more densely populated. Still, he said, their situation was better than those who lived in unrecognized villages, populated by Palestinians who remained inside the '48 boundaries but without legal status. Officially referred to in Israel as "present absentees," they were disadvantaged even more.

A tour outside the city led us to the proposed route of the "separation barrier/fence" that was to be built. Accompanied by a patrol of IDF soldiers, I was asked by one, "Do you think we are the evil conquerors?" I responded that I believed that people wanted to find a way to live in peace. "The Palestinian leadership has failed to rein in terrorism," he replied. "Palestinians we have talked with also want reform," I answered. We parted with his warning to me: "Keep your eyes open."

On our last day of the tour, we traveled to Karnei Shomron, an Israeli settlement near Nablus, deep inside the northern West Bank. To get there, we had to transfer from our bus to an armored Israeli bus. As we traversed the occupied Palestinian countryside on the way to the settlement, Tony Bing pointed to a distant Palestinian village and said it was Kafr Qasim, site of a massacre of the villagers by IDF forces in 1956.

At the settlement, established in 1977, we were met by Sondra Baras, an émigré from Cleveland in the '80s who was the director of an organization called Christian Friends of Israeli Communities, a program linking Christian Zionist congregations in the U.S. with Jewish settlements in the occupied territories.

Baras welcomed us to "Western Israel." When one of our group members asked if she didn't mean "Eastern Israel," implying that the West Bank was part of Israel, she responded, "No, I mean Western Israel. God gave all this land to us, including what lies across the Jordan River as the current Hashemite Kingdom of Jordan. In 1948 we Jews made an historic compromise by accepting the ceding of that land in addition to one-half of what rightfully belonged to us west of the Jordan River. We will not give any of the rest of it away." She went on to say, though, that if Palestinians would accept the coastal plain, including the cities of Tel Aviv and Haifa, "They are welcome to those; that was never part of biblical Israel. Judea and Samaria (the West Bank), however, is! We will never relinquish this."

One of the group members asked Baras if she were aware of the nature of Christian Zionism's theology and how they supported Israel and the '67 occupation because of their End Times theology—a theology that requires Israel's control of the region, including Jerusalem, so that the temple can be rebuilt and Jesus can come again. "But that theology also holds that when Jesus returns, there will be a terrible battle, and all who do not convert to Christianity will be slaughtered, including Jews."

Baras laughed and said, "Oh, yes. I know that. But we can't be too choosey about who our friends are. Besides, among those of us in the settlement movement, we have a little joke. When the Messiah comes, we will have a question for him: 'Is this your first or second visit?'"

Back in Jerusalem after our time away—and at the end of our tour—we spent nearly five hours processing all we had learned and preparing an epistle about our experience, a preliminary to the longer and harder work by a sub-group of producing the book that would become *When the Rain Returns: Toward Justice and Reconciliation in Palestine and Israel*. We were not overly optimistic and somewhat constrained by a sense that we could not publish our true feelings: that justice and reconciliation were a long way off, and that something more radical than a two-state solution was called for.

I left Jerusalem for my next stop, a work camp with Guilford students in Kenya. My anti-malarial Larium had not produced any anxiety. If I had any, it was about prospects for peace in the Middle East—and Jane's continuing life under curfew in Ramallah.

Chapter 7: The Second Intifada, Part 3

2003

In February of 2003 I was invited to participate in yet another tour. This time it was organized by Friends United Meeting, the international Quaker organization responsible for the Friends School in Ramallah. The Intifada had put the school in a precarious position, and FUM wanted a delegation of twenty-nine Friends from the United States and Kenya to visit and learn about the situation.

Although it had been less than a year since my last visit, I was surprised by the changes around Jerusalem. A Menachem Begin Heritage Center and Museum had been constructed very near our accomodations at St. Andrew's Hospice in West Jerusalem; a superhighway passed in front of Jaffa Gate—an area I remembered as no man's land in the early '70s; an Israeli nightclub was just below St. Andrews, humorously called "The Gates of Hell," as it was at the beginning of the Valley of Gihon, biblical *Gahenna*. But other sights were familiar: the King David Hotel just to the west; a spectacular view towards the hills of Moab in Jordan to the east; the old city walls of Jerusalem to the north.

On our first day, we oriented ourselves with a tour of the Old City, walking through the various quarters to the Western Wall, the *Kotel*. On the way there, we stopped at a Syrian Orthodox church which claimed to occupy the spot of the upper room, the place where Jesus held his last supper with the disciples. Through the Christian and Armenian Quarters, we noticed Israeli flags flying outside apartments showing how many settlers had moved beyond the Jewish Quarter.

Back at St. Andrews, I gave the group a brief overview of the current situation in Palestine and Israel, borrowing from Naomi Chazan's description of "two narratives that are both true—but don't meet." They would soon enough see it for themselves.

The next morning we heard from a representative of the Israeli Committee Against Home Demolitions (ICAHD). She spoke of 10,000 Palestinian homes demolished by Israel since 1967, some because of alleged connections with militants, some to make way for Israeli construction, but most because the owners didn't have the proper building permits—permits, we were told, that are almost impossible for Palestinians to procure.

We then took a tour to see one of the homes being rebuilt by ICAHD north of Jerusalem in Anata, biblical Anatoth, the home of the prophet Jeremiah. Saleem, the owner, described how his family's small home had been destroyed three times already. Israel deemed it too close to a planned settler road. That evening we heard a panel that included the founder of ICAHD, Jeff Halper; Palestinian human rights lawyer Jonathan Kuttab; and Arik Ascherman, executive director of Rabbis for Human Rights. Each described the challenging circumstances of the times but expressed optimism and hope.

The next day we went to Bethlehem. Although only a few miles south of Jerusalem and its apparently bustling commerce, Bethlehem seemed like a ghost town. Three years into the Intifada, the city had not only endured a deadly siege by the IDF, it was also suffering economically. There was an eighty percent unemployment rate in a city dependent on tourism. Our FUM group appeared to be the only one visiting, and desperate vendors followed us everywhere, begging us to buy their trinkets. We were mobbed as we entered the Church of the Nativity, and they waited for us as we toured not only the grotto traditionally associated with the birth of Jesus but also viewed the bullet marks from IDF snipers who surrounded the church and the 250 Palestinians seeking refuge there during the siege.

When we got on our bus to travel to the next site, they hopped in their cars and followed us there. Some of our members nearly emptied their wallets and purses in buying out of sympathy. While the souvenir sellers waited outside, we toured Sister Rose Mesa's Holy Family Center for Traumatized Children and learned of the terrible cost of the conflict on children. In spite of their trauma, however, the children sang beautifully for us.

Followed again by the vendors, we did some shopping in the few olive wood stores still open, ate at a restaurant, and viewed from a distance the site of Sir Moses Montefiore's homage to Rachel—her tomb. It was not accessible to us, however. It had been completely enclosed by Israel for security reasons and was now open only for Jews.

That evening at the hospice we met with Ira Kerem, an Israeli who shared how he had been a leftist and optimistic about peace with the Palestinians but was now distressed after more than two years of violence. "The left has vanished in Israel," he said. He was still opposed to the settlements, but he didn't think they were the impediment to peace—it was the Palestinians. Repeating the Israeli position, he cited Palestinian rejection of "Barak's generous offer," Arab antisemitism, constant violence, and the threat of terror. After the hopeful panel of the night before, it was a sober reminder of the mood in Israel in this second Intifada.

But that wasn't the last word of the evening. Following supper, we heard from Naim Ateek, the Anglican clergyman and founder of Sabeel, the Palestinian Liberation Theology Center. He was as adamant that Israel was at fault for not being a partner for peace as Kerem was about laying the blame at the feet of Arafat and the Palestinians. One member of our group, a Jewish Quaker, was having none of it, and the conversation grew quite tense, neither person giving ground.

When we finally traveled to Ramallah, it was good to see familiar places and faces. Former colleagues and students, the mother of a Guilford College student, and staff and students of the school greeted us as we arrived. The students led us around the campus, showing us the renovated classrooms, the USAid-funded new construction of a library/assembly hall/computer center building, and a German-funded natural area of indigenous trees and plants on the Swift House property—a lovely garden where my beloved dog Shatra was buried in '72.

That night, I took leave from the group to have supper with the family that had hosted Jane the previous summer during the military curfew. I enjoyed meeting with those old friends and my former housemate in Swift House, Donn Hutchison. Before the meal, the father of the family suggested that we drive through the city to see some of the sights, especially the headquarters of the Palestinian Authority, the *Muqata'a*. It was the old British Mandate fortress that later served the Jordanians and then the Israelis. It was now not only the Palestinian governmental headquarters, it was the residence of President Yasser Arafat.

And it was largely destroyed. During Israel's invasion of the year before, tanks, attack helicopters, and bulldozers wreaked havoc on it. Most of the complex was reduced to rubble. Yet all around it, homes and businesses had been quickly repaired. As in Israel after a bombing, people moved quickly to clean up and rebuild as a sign of resilience and refusal to be defeated. But the rubble surrounding Arafat was left as another sign: of the solidarity of the Palestinian governmental leaders with the people's suffering.

Returning to the house, my host exclaimed as he got out of his car, "That was wonderful! That was as far as I've been from home in almost three years!" We had traveled all of four miles. That, as I'd been told often, was about the extent of the Palestinian cantons carved out of the West Bank by the Oslo Accords.

Before going inside the house, however, the father wanted to show me what had happened to his garden and yard during the invasion. An Israeli bulldozer had destroyed his stone wall to use the materials as a blockade on the road leading to the *Muqata'a*. Along with the stone rubble, it had also taken much of his dirt and many of his beloved fruit trees. As soon as the

Israelis left, he rebuilt the wall, filled in as much of the yard as he could, and even rescued one of the olive trees, sticking it defiantly back in the earth. Like its owners, it is still surviving.

Over a delicious traditional dinner of *sfeeha*, *diwali*, and *cousa*, the family told me about the time Jane was with them under curfew—and how she helped relieve them of the boredom of being sequestered for days on end. They also told of how they remained under curfew even while other parts of the city weren't, as they were so close to the governmental complex. One of the areas nearby that had the curfew lifted was where the Friends School Upper School was located. With classes again meeting, their son wanted to attend, but there was a tank in their front yard and patrolling soldiers enforcing the curfew. The boy would time the patrols, wait for the turret of the tank to turn, and dash out the back door, over an adjoining wall, and through an open field to get to school.

Their daughter, who had been among the students to assist us on our '97 and '99 work camps, had graduated and wanted to attend college—but the parents were concerned about her safety in Palestine. We talked about Guilford, and the following year she enrolled.

The next day, our group toured the Lower School—the former Girls School. Like the Upper School, the former Boys School campus, its facilities had been vastly improved and expanded. The children sang for us and performed a funny skit.

Later we toured the Friends play center in the Amari refugee camp. Violet Zaru, the local Quaker who founded the center, met with us along with the two conservative Muslim teachers. The center served five-year-olds, at least fifty each year. During their year at the center, they were given a respite from the grim reality of life in the camp.

On a trip to a school for the blind, two teenage students read essays and poems to us from Braille texts. The language was strong and passionate about how fearful they had been from the shelling and shooting from the settlement just above their school. They also expressed their sense of injustice in how the U.S. had attacked Iraq for occupying Kuwait while Israel had occupied their land for more than thirty-five years.

Back at the Upper School, students gave us a performance of traditional Arabic music and *debke*. The folklore dance of Palestine, the *debke* had not been performed during the period of self-imposed mourning when I taught at the school. Now it was being performed as a passionate and beautiful expression of patriotism, connection to the land, and nonviolent resistance. I wished that it could be the face of Palestinians the world saw rather than suicide bombers.

At both campuses and on the streets, we had a lot of interaction with young people. While they appeared quite happy—and several even joked about how I looked with my long, gray beard and Arabic *keffiyeh*—they were also obviously concerned about the situation and their future. Nevertheless, they felt that they had it much better than others in Gaza, Nablus, Jenin, Hebron, and the villages.

As our group shared with the students and others in Ramallah about our experience elsewhere in Palestine and Israel, they expressed surprise and delight that there were such groups in Israel as Rabbis for Human Rights and ICAHD. "Why have we never heard of these groups?" they asked us. One of the parents at the school shared that in his work in the Palestinian Interior Ministry he had occasion to meet with similar functionaries in Israeli ministries. They can find agreement on many issues, but the "political hacks"—as he called them—at higher levels are locked into policy positions.

When we went to see the meetinghouse property, I was delighted to see that international fundraising had provided the resources to repair the meetinghouse roof and begin renovations. The plaster had been chipped off the stone walls, and new wiring and a heating system were being installed. We circled together with local Friends and had a time of silent worship, with many sharing out of the silence in spoken word or hymns such as "A Song of Peace." One in our group, the clerk of Philadelphia Yearly Meeting, was especially moved, as PYM had provided the first $50,000 toward the renovations after a speech at their annual sessions by Jean Zaru.

In a meeting with the executive leadership of the school, we were told of their commitment to ensuring the maintenance of the Quaker Christian values of the school, supported by the families and staff of the Friends School—even with a majority Muslim faculty, staff, and student body. Given the circumstances of the Intifada, they were challenged in covering expenses. While Ramallah was better off than other areas of the West Bank, and most students came from wealthy or middle class families, there were still only seventy-five percent who could be depended on to pay the school fees. Salaries of government workers were sporadic, and business and commerce were subject to the frequent closures and the economic hardship on the population.

It was hard to leave Ramallah and my old friends as we returned to Jerusalem for our final day of the trip. But I would soon see several of the young people—not on a subsequent work trip, but at Guilford! Several families met with me to talk about sending their children. Half a dozen would arrive over the next couple of years.

On that last day in Jerusalem, I wandered the familiar streets once more, memories coming in waves as they did in Ramallah. We had a final meeting as a group to discuss our takeaways—nothing concrete, but a commitment to support the school, play center, and Quaker community. All took away a deep affection for the people we met and several would return in the coming years.

2004

Our 2004 service-learning trip took on a different aspect as we co-planned and directed it with my Guilford faculty colleague, philosophy professor Rabbi Jonathan Malino. We gathered the group first at the Beit Shmuel hostel of Hebrew Union College in West Jerusalem. Our first night's discussions got us right into controversial matters: Jewish philosophy and a recent Supreme Court of Israel decision that the route of the "security fence/separation wall" was illegal in places.

On our first full day, we toured the Old City and then met with Jewish scholar Moshe Halbertal. He spoke with us about Israel's five main groups: Ultra-Orthodox Jews, secularists, Arab Jews, Russian emigrants, and Israeli Arabs. The Israeli

Arabs and "Ultras," he said, had opted out of helping form the society, thus forcing the other three groups to create the identity of a Jewish democracy acceptable to all. To maintain that democracy, he went on to say, would require a two-state solution.

As we continued our stay in Jerusalem, we joined a tour of the Western Wall tunnel, the angry response to which scuttled our first attempt at a work trip to Palestine and Israel in the early '90s. It was fascinating to get even closer to the foundation wall Herod had constructed for the second Jerusalem temple. Some of the Herodian stone weighed hundreds of tons and was placed several stories high in the eight-story high wall. Also impressive were the prayer niches along the tunnel where the devout could be even closer to the "Holy of Holies" of the temple, the residence of God on earth as believed by the faithful. Even with the temple's total destruction, they took scripture at its word that God's Presence would never leave Jerusalem.

As we exited the tunnel onto the Via Dolorosa in the Muslim Quarter, our guide told us to stay together as a group to await armed guards who would escort us out of the "dangerous" area. Much to the amazement of the others in the tour group, our contingent walked away, refusing the armed accompaniment.

Later in the day we met with the deputy director of the United Jewish Agency, an organization that helps immigrants settle in Israel. Along with describing the process of working with more than one million Ethiopian Jews who had arrived in Israel since 1990, she expressed her trepidation about our going to Ramallah. For her, as for many Israelis, Ramallah was identified as a terrorist haven and site of the lynching of two Israeli soldiers in the first months of the second Intifada. In Ramallah, one gets a different version of the story.

The day ended with a visit to the home of Tova Hartman, a friend of the Malinos who had established the world's first Orthodox, feminist synagogue. She shared with us her vision for the *schul*: a renewed Jewish spirituality that is not so focused on academics or the Talmud.

More adventures in Jerusalem included a tour of the Marc Chagall windows at the Hadassah Hospital and a visit to Yad Vashem, the Holocaust museum. Our guide, a political leftist, expressed to us her discomfort with what she described as the propagandistic nature of the museum's political purposes. After Yad Vashem, we visited the archaeological site at the Southern wall of the *Kotel* complex. Going down to the street level of Jesus's day, the site clearly demonstrated the enormity of Herod's grandiose plans for the temple, and I couldn't help but recall Jesus's prediction of its demise—and his refusal to be impressed by it.

The visit to the eight-story high foundation wall of the temple site was followed by a visit to the modern-day wall Israel had built around Jerusalem. The portion we saw served no apparent security purpose. The twenty-six-foot-high concrete structure went right down the middle of a main street of Abu Dis, the Arab suburb in which the Palestinians had begun building their legislative buildings. Cutting the village off from Jerusalem effectively ended the possibility that it could serve as the "Jerusalem capital" of a future Palestinian state.

Israel's separation barrier, "the wall," constructed down the middle of one of the main streets of Abu Dis.

That evening, we met with another Jewish scholar, Yehuda Gellman, who told us that he saw no good solution coming out of the current conflict, although he felt a two-state solution would be fair. "But it would be a terror state," he said. "The wall is OK, as it prevents the loss of Jewish life even if it causes hardships for the Palestinians." Later that evening with another Jewish scholar, Avishai Margalit, we heard a differing opinion. He viewed the wall as a political act on the part of the Israeli government and firmly believed that Arafat had not started the second Intifada, contradicting the popular opinion that the Palestinian leader had rejected the peace process, believing he could gain more by violence.

After such intense academically-oriented discussions, it was a change of pace to meet with another friend of the Malinos, Maya Bar-Hillel. A professor of cognitive psychology, she had done a statistical analysis of the popular book *The Bible Code*, debunking the belief that the Bible included encrypted prophecies in its pages. She explained how the same prophecies could be found in the pages of *War and Peace*. But she also described her work with Maqsom Watch, a group of women who monitor the Israeli checkpoints to try to prevent abuse of Palestinians.

Bar-Hillel's daughter, Gili, then shared with us her work translating *Harry Potter* into Hebrew. A young graduate student, she was hired to do the work on the first book when nobody knew it would be so popular. She tackled the task of deciding whether to transliterate or translate into equivalencies in Hebrew culture. She chose the latter.

Our time in Jerusalem concluded with a visit to the Supreme Court of Israel, the Israel Museum, and the Shrine of the Book. In the new Supreme Court building, we contemplated the intentional architectural features designed to symbolize biblical themes of "circles of justice," "straight paths," and "justice at the gates." As the trip continued and we heard continued narratives of life there, we often thought back on how well incorporated those themes were in a building, but not as well in practice.

As we transitioned from Jerusalem and an emphasis on the Jewish Israeli narrative to the Palestinian one, we traveled up the Mediterranean coast to the Galilee. On the way, we stopped at the Roman ruins of Caesarea with its amphitheater, remains of Pilate's former home, the hippodrome, aqueducts, and an ancient port. We also toured the old Crusader port of Acre and a museum dedicated to the Warsaw Ghetto fighters. At the museum, I was struck by the parallels between tactics used by the Jewish resistance—and their later vital role in the establishment of the state of Israel—and the tactics used by the Palestinian resistance.

Settling in for two days in Ibillin at the Mar Elias Educational Institute, we were surprised by a visit from Abuna Elias Chacour, now Archbishop of Galilee and typically in residence at his office in Haifa. He showed us the nearly completed Church of the Beatitudes on the school's grounds and invited us for conversation at his old home. He shared with us his worries about Israel's cuts in educational subsidies to Arab schools and his sadness over the fact that Jewish students stopped coming to Mar Elias with the start of the Intifada. He was hoping, though, for good to come from a six-month exchange program with a Jewish school.

After a day touring religious sites around the Sea of Galilee—and even taking a swim (looking to see who, in proper holiness, couldn't break the surface)—we headed back south by way of the Church of the Annunciation in Nazareth and a tour of the archaeological digs at Har Megiddo, biblical Armageddon. We were told of the proposed plan by the Department of Tourism in 1999 to put up surveillance cameras to capture the event in case Jesus returned at Y2K. Wiser minds prevailed, and the idea was not adopted.

Back in Jerusalem, we attended Friday night services at Tova Hartman's Orthodox, feminist synagogue before heading to Bethlehem the next day. The service showed how creatively they had melded Orthodox traditions with progressive, feminist inclusivity even in their definition of a *minyan*, the Jewish quorum required to hold worship, as not just ten men, but also ten women.

In Bethlehem, we witnessed how creatively another woman, Nuha Khoury, had helped to create a cultural center at the Christmas Lutheran Church to address the trauma experienced by the children of the Intifada. A lovely building had been constructed with $5 million in Finnish Lutheran funds, and Nuha told us of the programs of the Dar Annadwa Center that addressed the needs of the children with film, theater, art, and other enrichment activities. The focus of the programs was to instill hope in the future rather than to dwell on the horrors of the past. In that vein, one of the art programs had the children collect the broken glass in the streets resulting from the invasions and turn it into stained glass angels, candles, and other objects. Needless to say, we nearly bought them out of the lovely items in the center's gift shop.

Finally in Ramallah, we worshiped with Friends in the beautifully restored meetinghouse on Sunday and took a walking tour of Ramallah and El-Bireh. Our first work day had us clearing brush and preparing for a major painting job of the wall around the new soccer field. But little could prepare us for our first program: attendance at a ceremony at the governmental headquarters, the *Muqata'a*, presided over by Yasser Arafat himself.

I could hardly recognize the governmental complex. It was still mostly bombed out from the Israeli siege, and there were now hundreds of flattened cars piled around the grounds— remnants from the joy riding of Israeli tanks through the streets during the invasions. The only buildings left unscathed were an assembly hall, Arafat's apartment, and a barracks or two. We gathered with a large crowd in the assembly hall, and then Arafat entered.

A short man, dressed in olive drab, he strode to the dais in the front of the room and sat with an assemblage of Christian and Muslim clergy. He continually adjusted his carefully arranged *keffiyeh* and fiddled with the medals on his jacket. He spoke only briefly, addressing his delight in Muslim/Christian relations and ending with, "Next time in Jerusalem." I noted in my journal that he looked well and didn't tremble as much as I'd seen on TV back in the U.S. Only four months later he would be dead.

Over the next two days we met with Ghassan Khatib, Minister of Labor in the Palestinian Authority; president of Al-Quds University, Sari Nusseibeh; and political scientist Ali Jirbawi. Khatib expressed his disappointment in the United States' rejection of an international court's ruling against Israel's wall, saying it encouraged the more violent element in Palestinian society. Nusseibeh told us of his work with Israeli Ami Ayalon on an alternative peace plan and the "million and one little signs of hope" he saw. Jirbawi described the creation of the Palestinian Authority as Israel's "trick" to deny citizenship to the Palestinians in the occupied territories. "But we will still be here," he said. "The unorganized always win out over the organized."

After a dinner for prospective Guilford students at the restaurant of a Guilford family, we met with another Guilford family at their apartment. They told us of how their daughter had been used as a human shield during the 2002 Israeli invasion. Awakened in the middle of the night by the soldiers, the girl was taken door to door throughout the apartment complex to knock and call on residents to open up. Perhaps the experience set her on her career path. After she graduated from Guilford with a psychology major, she went on to earn a Ph.D. in clinical psychology.

In conversations with various people in Ramallah, I also got the alternative narrative about the lynchings so many in Israel associate with Ramallah. In the Israeli version, two IDF reservists took the wrong turn on their way to their unit in the West Bank, wound up in Ramallah, and were overwhelmed by a mob, hauled into the police station next to the Upper School campus of the Friends School, eviscerated, and tossed out of a second floor window. The Ramallah version is that they were two plain clothes spies, parked in a car at the front gate of the Friends School as a funeral procession for a peasant killed by settlers passed by. Recognized by their listening devices, the two were mobbed by angry mourners, but Palestinian police intervened and took them into the station for safety. However, the enraged mourners were in such large numbers that they overwhelmed the police, killed the two Israelis, and tossed their bodies out the window.

Within an hour of the incident, an Israeli attack helicopter fired two rockets into the station, destroying it. In a later attack, eight rockets were fired into the remains of the building, completely leveling it, and damaging the Friends School next door.

The Palestinian police station after Israeli rockets hit it the first time.

After the rocket attack, the police approached Violet Zaru, a member of Ramallah Friends Meeting, to say that they were planning to take over half of her and her sister's home as a temporary police station. The home, a former soap factory, was large enough that half was a residence, and half had been used as a school, but was then empty. Violet, fearing what could happen to the whole building should Israel decide to strike the police again, asked a nephew what to do. That night the nephew arranged for a bulldozer to destroy the vacant half of the building.

In addition to painting, clearing brush, and clearing trash from the site of the ancient Byzantine church where we had worked on a previous trip, we also did a work day at the Amari Play Center Violet had started. While sharing with us about the mission of the center to offer a year of "normalcy" for children in the middle of such abnormal circumstances, Violet told us, "When I die, I want to tell God something: 'If you plan on making another world some day, don't repeat the mistake of putting three of your great prophets of different religions in the same place!'"

Our last few days in Ramallah included a lot of painting of window grates and railings and many conversations about the political situation. Adel Yahya, director of the Palestinian Association for Cultural Exchange, also repeated a common belief: "We don't see an end game yet; everyone knows what the solution is, but leadership on both sides is too corrupt to get us there."

Yasser Abed Rabbo, Arafat's former press secretary, shared with us about his and Israeli Yossi Beilin's peace plan, "The Geneva Initiative." "As a refugee myself," he told us, "it was hard for me to compromise on the 'right of return' in our plan, but both sides have to do hard things if we are to find a solution."

We also met with families who had students at Guilford and those about to attend, including the son of a former student of mine when I taught in Ramallah. His mother evidently had forgiven me for my bad teaching, as we had an amazing meal under the olive and almond trees in their back yard in Birzeit. The young man's father was the town's mayor, and he shared how the town was half Muslim and half Christian, and all got along wonderfully. He also said that he hoped for the same co-existence one day between Israelis and Palestinians.

On our way back to Ramallah, only a few miles distant, we experienced one of the major complaints of Palestinians under occupation: the randomness of travel restrictions. Both Birzeit and Ramallah are in Area A, territories under the control of the Palestinian Authority, but Israel insisted in the Oslo Accords to have a narrow strip of the highway between the two municipalities designated Area C—under total Israeli control. Israel could close the highway at any time they wished, and often did. That night, they did. We were caught in a massive traffic backup as Israeli soldiers wove in and out of the line-up. We heard shots fired, but we never learned what was the cause of the stoppage. Drivers remained calm and were even joking with each other and with us. Finally the cars began moving, and the "flying checkpoint" was open once more.

As always, it was hard to leave Ramallah when the time came, especially with the sincere expressions of gratitude to us for sharing in the experience of those we were leaving behind. But we had two final days of the trip ahead of us, and we returned to Jerusalem. Back at Beit Schmuel we met with Ruthi Gavison, a leading Israeli legal authority. After the somewhat optimistic impression we got in Ramallah about Palestinian hopes for the future, the group was disappointed to hear Gavison's justification of the wall's being erected largely on Palestinian land, of the illegality of the settlements but opposition to removing them, and of the impossibility that Jews would remain in a future Palestinian state, as "Palestinians can't be trusted, and it would be too dangerous."

On our last day, we rose early and traveled to the Dead Sea Valley to visit Jericho, the Dead Sea Scrolls community of Qumran, and Masada. I was surprised by the number of new excavations at Masada and by Jonathan Malino's description of how the "Zealots' stronghold" was becoming less and less a part of Israel's mythology as the state developed other stories of persistence—and research continued to call into question the historicity of the familiar story of the Zealots' resistance.

Also intriguing at Masada was the presence of a new cable car system that offered easier access to the top of the rock plateau than the Romans' dirt ramp and the "snake path" up the side. As we climbed onto the large gondola for the ascent, we were joined by an American church group whose pastor told them solemnly as the car began to move, "I want you to know that while we are in the air, God will not be with us." He paused for the effect of his words to sink in, and then he explained why: "It says in the Bible, 'Lo, I am with you always.'"

We made it up and back down OK, however. And we made it to the airport that night and through security with the usual extensive luggage search once we informed the staff that we had been in the Palestinian territories.

2005

In March of 2005, Jane, Maia, and I joined a number of other Quakers with a keen interest in the work of Friends in Ramallah for the joyous re-dedication of the restored meetinghouse. Following a two-year renovation overseen by Jean Zaru's engineer son Walid and funded by donations from Quakers from around the world, the historic 1910 building was again ready to serve Friends in Ramallah and beyond.

Plaster had been stripped off the interior walls, exposing the beautiful Jerusalem limestone used in constructing the solid stone walls. A new roof, new wiring, and even a heating system were installed. Our work camp in 2004 had planted numerous trees—including olive, eucalyptus, and pine. The building and surroundings were once again lovely. As we gathered for worship, the walls reverberated with familiar hymns and messages out of the silence reflected on what that space had meant to people over the years. There were many tears, but even more smiles. Jews, Christians, and Muslims were among the one hundred in attendance and attested to the importance of Friends in the cultural and religious life of the region. Ramallah's mayor shared how, though not a Quaker himself, he enjoyed attending Sunday school led by Ellen Mansur along with hundreds of other young people.

Ramallah Friends meetinghouse after restoration, trees planted by our work camps visible on the grounds.

Donn Hutchison noted that the rededication was occurring ninety-five years to the day from the original March 6, 1910 dedication of the meetinghouse. A photo of that occasion was displayed in the worship room and showed a large crowd gathered outside the new building, including Timothy Hussey, the New England Quaker who had supervised the construction. Surrounding the building was open countryside, a stark contrast to the noisy, busy commercial center that now encompassed the little oasis of the Friends meetinghouse and grounds.

After the rededication ceremonies, we joined a group of Friends to discuss how the work of the Quaker community in Ramallah could be supported and the meetinghouse used for the benefit of others. The political and economic situation in the area had resulted in an exodus of much of the Christian community, including Quakers, and there were few Friends remaining to maintain the vibrancy of the meeting's work. In addition to our own conversations, we met with a variety of Palestinians and Israelis to seek their advice about how the continuing Quaker presence in Ramallah could be beneficial to all.

In Jerusalem we met with Naim Ateek and Samia Khoury of Sabeel, the Palestinian Liberation Theology Center. They urged us to work for encouraging Christian-Muslim relations, maintaining a Christian community in the Holy Land, supporting Palestinian peace and justice efforts, and partnering with Sabeel itself. Gila Svirsky, an Israeli Jew active with other women in the peace movement, met with us in the West Jerusalem office of Bat Shalom and told us of the coordinated efforts of Israeli and Palestinian women working for an end to the occupation—but shared how difficult those efforts were with the increased separation between Israel and the occupied territories and the shrinking since 2000 of the Israeli "peace camp."

In Hebron, we visited the university and were told of the use of education increasingly as "the weapon of choice" in ending the occupation. Staff also expressed their concern that the ongoing occupation was harming the image of Islam in the world. Later, we traveled to the Muslim village of At-Tuwani to learn about their efforts of nonviolent resistance to the atrocities of a neighboring Israeli settlement.

A panel of representatives from various Palestinian peace groups met with us in Bethlehem and told us of their efforts in bringing internationals to the region to show them the "facts on the ground," using technology and news media in getting the word out about their efforts, offering training opportunities in nonviolence theory and practice, and empowering youth through education and cultural activities. They encouraged the use of the Friends meetinghouse as a center for dialogue and reconciliation. Also, in Bethlehem, we met with Mitri Raheb, pastor of the Christmas Lutheran Church. He led us on a tour of facilities used for arts enrichment, youth activities, vocational training, and programs for introducing tourists to the "living stones" of Palestine rather than the "dead stones" of ancient edifices.

As a result of the consultation, a new organization, the Friends International Center in Ramallah, was formed with the intent of providing financial and spiritual support for the work of Friends in Ramallah and the cultural aspirations of the broader community in Palestine—and to promote a just peace in Palestine and Israel.

Returning to Palestine and Israel a few months later on our summer service-learning trip, I anticipated several exciting additions to our planned experience. The first of those was a Jewish Quaker Guilford student on a first trip into the Palestinian territories after extensive experience in Israel. In fact, she was joining us in Ramallah following a visit to family on a kibbutz.

I went to Jerusalem to accompany her as she joined our group, and I couldn't help but be amused by her first lesson in how different two cultures are that live side by side. Dressed in typical college student and secular Israeli attire, she asked if she should cover up a little. I affirmed that she should. As we boarded the Arab bus for Ramallah, she noticed how conservatively dressed other women were and added another layer. By the time we arrived in Ramallah, only her face was visible.

We joined the group for a tour of Ramallah and El-Bireh led by Adel Yahya of PACE. In addition to viewing many of the usual sites, we toured an area where Palestinian Authority leaders lived in palatial homes. Adel was clearly upset by the lavish lifestyle of the leadership, and I was not surprised as he reiterated his disgust with the corruption rife in the PA.

But I was surprised by the changes elsewhere. The burned-over no-man's land we had viewed in 2001 was refurbished. Land on either side of the formerly blackened street was being tilled by peasant farmers, and an abandoned hotel was being renovated.

The surprise continued at the governmental headquarters, the *Muqata'a*. During our visit the previous summer to hear an address by Yasser Arafat, the complex was in ruins. Only months after Arafat's death, the piles of flattened cars were gone, the rubble was cleared, and buildings were being renovated. Although Arafat's open air tomb was clearly a place of veneration, the refurbished campus was a clear sign that new leadership was interested in presenting a different face to the world.

There was no surprise, though, in the pessimism expressed by a familiar speaker to our groups, Ghassan Khatib. Now Minister of Planning in the PA, he spoke to us of the problem with Prime Minister Sharon's disengagement plan for Gaza. "Israel is doing this unilaterally without consultation with the Palestinians," he told us. "Besides, they will continue to control Gaza's borders, so the Strip will still be occupied in reality." He went on to tell us that the spread of settlements was rapidly causing the window of opportunity to close on a two-state solution. While the PA continued to move forward with the Bush Administration's roadmap for peace, Israel was ignoring it. "This is strengthening Hamas," Khatib said. "In an election, they will win many protest votes."

At supper with a Guilford family, we gained a sense of growing normalcy as the uprising waned. The mother shared stories of the terror of the 2002 Israeli incursion—including her own daughter being used as a human shield—but told with the kind of humor that distance can afford. She spoke also of her concern for the young Israeli soldiers as well as for Palestinian youth and told of how soldiers allowed her to pass through a checkpoint to get to Jerusalem to buy her daughter a prom dress. They were genuinely interested in seeing the dress when she returned through the checkpoint.

Another supper with the Guilford family in Birzeit was not only as delightful as the summer before; it also gave us opportunity to see further evidence of reduced tension. Returning to Ramallah through the place where a "flying checkpoint" held up traffic the previous year, we saw no evidence of Israeli presence. We flew through.

Other normalcy was found in our work assignments of painting railings and window grates. As usual, the paint was almost as thin as water. It covered not only the metal but also the limestone facades, our clothes, and our appendages.

For the first time in several years, we were able to meet with Hanan Ashrawi, long out of her position in the PA and heading an NGO that worked to develop democratic institutions in the Palestinian territories. She had turned down a meeting with the president of the European Union to be with us. Most of her hour and a half with us, however, was dedicated to a critique of the Bush administration and the neo-conservatives in it who were pushing disastrous policies in the Middle East. Similar to Ghassan Khatib, she described Israel's disengagement from Gaza as detrimental to the roadmap.

Our meeting with Ashrawi was followed by one with Mustafa Barghouti, a medical doctor and presidential candidate who had received nineteen percent of the votes in the last election. He showed us a slide presentation on the ever-shrinking map of Palestine from the time of the British Mandate, through the UN partition plan and the establishment of the state of Israel, to the Oslo Accords and division of the Palestinian territories into Areas A, B, and C. He, too, believed the possibility of a two-state solution was rapidly disappearing.

A day in Jerusalem had us not only at many of the religious sites but also in meetings with a variety of Israeli peace activists. Rotem Mor shared with us about his decision to refuse induction into the Israeli military. There is no conscientious objector status in Israel, so he had to serve a prison sentence. Upon release he went to work with the American Friends Service Committee in Jerusalem. Nina Mayorek of Maqsom Watch shared how some Israeli checkpoints were being made more and more like international border crossings with modern terminals and electronic processing. It was making it more difficult to monitor human rights abuses at them. Gila Svirsky of Women in Black told us how they had to give up their weekly vigils in West Jerusalem because of violent threats against them. Staff at Rabbis for Human Rights shared about their ongoing work against settler destruction of Palestinian property.

On our way back to Ramallah, we experienced a little of the Palestinians' harassment at the checkpoints as some sort of incident had occurred, and traffic was moving very slowly. We finally got through but had to get a *service*, the public taxi, that could accommodate our group. There was room for one more passenger, and an elderly peasant woman in traditional clothing joined us. Recognizing us as Americans, and frustrated by her experience at the checkpoint, she entertained us with a long tirade in Arabic, none of which we could understand other than the periodic "Bush!" She was obviously not a fan.

We continued to enjoy dinner hospitality with Guilford families almost nightly, along with hosting our own recruiting dinner at Darna, the restaurant owned by one of the families. At one home, we heard from the father, a person tasked by the PA with the job of planning the rebuilding of Gaza following Israel's disengagement. He told us about another problem with Israel's unilateralism: he had received no word from Israel about what would be left standing, what destroyed, and what infrastructure would remain functioning. He had hired a corps of engineers, but he had no idea how to prepare them for the work ahead.

More speakers to the group in Ramallah included Yasser Abed Rabbo once more. He, too, criticized the Gaza pullout, citing its accomplishment without any negotiations as a bad sign that Sharon intended to push forward without including Palestinians in decision-making about the future. Still, he remained hopeful and spoke of Palestinians' long patience. Later at another Guilford student's home for dinner, we heard that Abed Rabbo was not overly popular among Palestinians because of his compromise on the "right of return" in his and Beilin's Geneva Initiative peace plan.

As we undertook our trip to the Galilee, we were joined by a family from Greensboro, North Carolina. The father was the pastor of a Presbyterian church, and the mother was a biblical scholar who was on study leave from her college and was serving as a scholar-in-residence at Tantur, the ecumenical study center in Bethlehem. Their insights and biblical knowledge added greatly to our experience.

Following our tour of the religious sites around the Sea of Galilee, we again went to Ibillin and volunteered a day's work at the Mar Elias School. We met once more with Abuna Elias Chacour, who emphasized that Jews and Arabs must learn to live together. As always, he was adamant about how unbalanced policies of the U.S. are in the region.

After the usual return to Ramallah by way of the Jordan Valley, we took a day to visit Bethlehem and Hebron. In Bethlehem we visited the Church of the Nativity, met with Nuha Khoury at Dar Annadwa, and stopped at the Holy Land Trust to talk with Husam Jubran. He told us of his conversion to nonviolence after his own violence in the first Intifada and subsequent arrest and jail time in Israel.

We met with Christian Peacemaker Teams workers in Hebron and witnessed the continuing impact of the settlers on the market area. More and more shops were closed. Hebrew graffiti on doors and walls called for "death to Arabs" and depicted the Prophet Mohammad as a pig writing the Qur'an. Following a brief tour of the affected part of Hebron, we traveled to the southern hills of the West Bank beyond Hebron to the village of At-Tuwani. CPT staff and other international peace activists were living in the primitive village of former nomadic Palestinians to help shield them from the depredations of a settlement on the hill above that was so violent it was deemed illegal even by Israel.

That very day, settlers had moved into the village's wheat fields with a harvester and stolen their entire crop. They had thrown dead chickens into the village's cistern, ruining their water source. Children had been attacked on their way to school. In spite of it all, the Muslim villagers remained nonviolent and gentle in spirit.

On our last night in Ramallah, we had our usual check-in with the group. The various participants shared how the experience had impacted them, and characteristically, described it as life changing, but wondered how they could adequately communicate the realities they had witnessed to skeptical folks back home. One student, the Jewish Quaker, remained rather quiet, saving her comments for a private conversation with me later.

After the rest of the group had left, she came to me and said, "Max, all my life I've heard from family members I love, teachers at my Hebrew school I love, and rabbis I love, that this land was empty until Jews came from Europe to settle it and 'make the desert bloom.' That's not true, is it?"

We had a good discussion about the competing narratives of the situation but that, in fact, Palestine was not empty before Israel's establishment. There were bustling Palestinian Arab cities, a vital Palestinian Arab culture, thriving Palestinian Arab institutions. "I know that now," she said. "What can I do about that back home?" We talked about the difficulties she would face in sharing a truth that others would deny. She maintained that she was up to the task and wanted to take it on. "I want to learn both Arabic and Hebrew," she told me, "so I can tell each other's stories."

To be sure, there are stories to tell.

Afterword

February of 2005 marked the end of the second Intifada and saw the beginning of Palestinian civil society's adoption of a variety of nonviolent tactics and strategies in resistance to the occupation. Succeeding years of work camps, personal visits, and academic programs would introduce me to some of the leaders of the new movements as well as to a growing variety of people in Palestine and Israel living in the ever-changing reality of their situation. Those experiences from 2005 to 2020 are the makings of yet another book, one leading to the fiftieth anniversary of Great-Aunt Annice's first warning to me in 1970 not to besmirch the good Carter name in Ramallah!

www.ingramcontent.com/pod-product-compliance
Lightning Source LLC
Chambersburg PA
CBHW070158100426
42743CB00013B/2961